The Earth Gives, the Earth Wants

Critical South

The publication of this series is supported by the International Consortium of Critical Theory Programs funded by the Andrew W. Mellon Foundation.

Series editors: Natalia Brizuela, Victoria J. Collis-Buthelezi and Leticia Sabsay

Mário Pinto de Andrade, *The Revolution Will be a Poetic Act*
Leonor Arfuch, *Memory and Autobiography*
Hélé Béji, *We, the Decolonized*
Maurits van Bever Donker, *Texturing Difference*
Paula Biglieri and Luciana Cadahia, *Seven Essays on Populism*
Antônio Bispo dos Santos, *The Earth Gives, the Earth Wants*
Sueli Carneiro, *Dispositif of Raciality*
Gisela Catanzaro, *Spectrology of Authoritarian Neoliberalism*
Aimé Césaire, *Resolutely Black*
Aimé Césaire, *Toussaint Louverture*
Victoria J. Collis-Buthelezi and Aaron Kamugisha (eds.), *The Caribbean Race Reader*
Bolívar Echeverría, *Modernity and "Whiteness"*
Diego Falconí Trávez, *From Ashes to Text*
Celso Furtado, *The Myth of Economic Development*
Eduardo Grüner, *The Haitian Revolution*
Francisco-J. Hernández Adrián, *On Tropical Grounds*
Ailton Krenak, *Ancestral Future*
Ailton Krenak, *Life is Not Useful*
Premesh Lalu, *Undoing Apartheid*
Karima Lazali, *Colonial Trauma*
María Pia López, *Not One Less*
Achille Mbembe and Felwine Sarr (eds.), *The Politics of Time*
Achille Mbembe and Felwine Sarr (eds.), *To Write the Africa World*
Valentin-Yves Mudimbe, *The Scent of the Father*
Pablo Oyarzun, *Doing Justice*
Néstor Perlongher, *Plebeian Prose*
Bento Prado Jr., *Error, Illusion, Madness*
Nelly Richard, *Eruptions of Memory*
Silvia Rivera Cusicanqui, *Ch'ixinakax utxiwa*
Suely Rolnik, *Spheres of Insurrection*
Rita Segato, *The War Against Women*
Tendayi Sithole, *The Black Register*
Maboula Soumahoro, *Black is the Journey, Africana the Name*
Fatou Sow, *Feminism in Africa*
Javad Tabatabai, *Ibn Khaldun and the Social Sciences*
Dénètem Touam Bona, *Fugitive, Where Are You Running?*

The Earth Gives, the Earth Wants

Antônio Bispo dos Santos

Translated by
Alex Brostoff and Jamille Pinheiro Dias

polity

Originally published in Portuguese as *A terra dá, a terra quer* © Ubu Editora / PISEAGRAMA, 2023.

Artwork © Santídio Pereira
Photos © João Liberato

Original Portuguese text:
Editorial coordination: PISEAGRAMA
Research and organization: Felipe Carnevalli, Fernanda Regaldo, Paula Lobato, Renata Marquez, Wellington Cançado
Editorial preparation: Fernanda Regaldo, Paula Lobato, Renata Marquez
Transcription: Emir Lucresia, Schelton Casimira
Editing: Daniela Uemura

Polity Press
65 Bridge Street
Cambridge CB2 1UR, UK

Polity Press
111 River Street
Hoboken, NJ 07030, USA

ISBN-13: 978-1-5095-7019-5 – hardback
ISBN-13: 978-1-5095-7020-1– paperback

A catalogue record for this book is available from the British Library.

Library of Congress Control Number: 2025951472

Typeset in 12.5 on 17 pt Sabon
by Fakenham Prepress Solutions, Fakenham, Norfolk NR21 8NL
Printed and bound in Great Britain by Ashford Colour Ltd

The publisher has used its best endeavors to ensure that the URLs for external websites referred to in this book are correct and active at the time of going to press. However, the publisher has no responsibility for the websites and can make no guarantee that a site will remain live or that the content is or will remain appropriate.

Every effort has been made to trace all copyright holders, but if any have been overlooked the publisher will be pleased to include any necessary credits in any subsequent reprint or edition.

For further information on Polity, visit our website:
politybooks.com

Mandacaru, xiquexique
Crown-of-friar and quipá
Macambira, *cat's claw*
Jurema *and* caroá
The thorns' beauty
Adorns the paths
Where I love to walk

Contents

Introduction

Territorial Autobiography

On Sunday, December 3, 2023, one week before he turned sixty-four, our dear friend the thinker Antônio Bispo dos Santos left the Earth[1] to journey beyond. He would object to being called a thinker, as he did so many times, and instead say he was a translator of worlds. Generous master of confluence, of organic knowledge and counter-colonialism, Bispo transformed and continues to radically transform our modes of thinking (and of living), of teaching (and of learning), of writing (and of speaking), and of imagining fruitful presents and other futures.

In 1996, the Zapatistas declared that we needed to learn to build a world where many worlds fit. This

---

[1] TR. Earth/earth: see p. 29, n. 1.

remains the great challenge we face when we consciously choose a way of life that runs counter to the deadly, monological, and persistent narrative of the heroic colonizer. Alongside many worlds, translation becomes a skill of vital importance. Rather than serving as a tool of extermination, domination, or betrayal, translation is reimagined as a sensitive act of moving through, living with, co-creating, and experimenting alongside other worlds; taking part, that is, in urgent and openly unexpected forms of creation.

Bispo was the first of his family to leave the Saco Curtume Quilombo[2] in Piauí to learn to read. He was given the mission of temporarily leaving his counter-colonial world – a world of orality and of ancient African cosmological paradigms that pre-date Brazil – to learn the colonizers' written language. After learning to read and write, the plan was that he would return to the *quilombo* and translate the legal landownership documents imposed by the State.

Our people's contracts were made orally, for our relationship with the land came through cultivation. The land did not belong to us; we belonged to the land.[3]

---

[2] TR. *Quilombo*: see p. 34, n. 5.
[3] Antônio Bispo dos Santos, "We Belong to the Land," *PISEAGRAMA Magazine,* December 2023 (https://piseagrama. org/in-english/we-belong-to-the-land-2/).

Bispo soon realized, however, that the mission first entrusted to him by his community was in fact far broader. Becoming a translator between worlds would place him in a constant state of movement, and it would put him in the role of giving poetic and cosmopolitical form to that passage. He saw that he could "turn the weapons of our enemies into a means of defense"[4] and embraced literacy as a way to counteract writing itself.

If they want me to move from orality to writing, I've been doing the opposite: I've been bringing writing back into orality.[5]

By countering the exclusionary dominance of the printed word, Bispo's approach to writing becomes a way to affirm the living presence of the *quilombola* ways of learning, passing on, and sharing knowledge. With his sharp play on words, he engaged in what he called a "war of names,"[6] a practice of counteracting colonial words as a way to weaken them. Writing was his way of oralizing the written word.

*

[4] See p. 22.
[5] Antônio Bispo dos Santos, manuscript to be published by PISEAGRAMA and Ubu in 2026.
[6] See p. 23.

This book is therefore born from orality.

A playful poet of family verse games formed through the oral traditions of the elders, Bispo used to tell us that what "the world lacked was poetry."[7] Édouard Glissant said something similar: that poetry was "the only thing able to connect the concert of the world to the fantasy of the world."[8] While Glissant's fantasy may well be called "creolization," Bispo's might be called *confluence*. In both of their journeys, whether through Glissant's Caribbean world or Bispo's Brazilian one, the desire for the "fantasy of the world" involves dreaming of worlds that refuse homogenization. They call for experimental, unpredictable configurations, shaped by organic encounters with heterogeneous elements. Like poetry itself, with all its creative maneuvers.

When we enter into confluence, we don't stop being ourselves; we become ourselves and other selves – we make space.[9]

To challenge literacy, to oralize writing, to give words world, body, struggle, poetry, and imagination: this was Bispo's shared way of reshaping writing and orality into

---

[7] Personal communication, March 2023.
[8] Édouard Glissant and Hans Ulrich Obrist, *Archipelago*, Rio de Janeiro: Isolarii, 2021, p. 132.
[9] See p. 25.

confluence. Bispo used to say he was "a landworker by essence" and "a writer by convenience."[10] Over time, writing, this act of convenience, refined itself into a specific practice of confluence for him.

The story of this book begins in 2021, when my team at PISEAGRAMA and I invited Bispo to join us for a series of conversations over the course of that year and the following.[11] While some conversations took place online, others, to our delight, took place in person. The confluence of orality and writing unfolded for us as a confluence of listening and writing. Speaking, listening, and writing were three simultaneous acts that transformed the *quilombo*'s messages into a traveling book made for other worlds. *The Earth Gives, the Earth Wants* thus emerged from writing in confluence, cultivated with affection and trust, yet constantly confronted by the translational challenge of this borderland between worlds, where we became ourselves and other selves.

[10] Personal communication, March 2023.
[11] The team at PISEAGRAMA, a publishing platform created in Belo Horizonte, Brazil, in 2010 and dedicated to imagining other possible worlds, was made up of the following members in 2022 and 2023 when the Portuguese edition of *The Earth Gives, the Earth Wants* was in production: Renata Marquez, Wellington Cançado, Fernanda Regaldo, Paula Lobato, Felipe Carnevalli, Emir Lucresia, and Shelton Casimira (https://piseagrama.org/in-english/).

In this way, the book was co-versed or conversed into being, as Marisol de la Cadena suggested while I was doing research in California in 2024. It was there, too, while standing on Indigenous land and in dialogue with Natalia Brizuela through Marisol, that I first encountered the English and Spanish translations of this traveling text.

We had already published essays by Bispo in our magazine in 2016 and 2018. The essays emerged through our method of researching, listening, writing, editing, and publishing in confluence; we called them "listening-writings (and vice versa)."[12] But the proposal for this book was new: to discuss architecture and spatiality in the *quilombo* and cities. How do the spaces produced in these two territories relate to one another? How might they reproduce, oppose, or contradict the idea of cosmophobia?

Bispo defined cosmophobia as a humanist illness, of those who don't see themselves as animals. He would say: "I'm not human. I am *quilombola*. I'm a landworker, a fisherman, a being of the cosmos."[13] And he would

---

[12] Renata Marquez, Wellington Cançado, Fernanda Regaldo, Paula Lobato, and Felipe Carnevalli (eds.), *Terra: Antologia Afro-indígena*, Belo Horizonte/São Paulo: PISEAGRAMA/UBU, 2023; available in English at https://piseagrama.org/in-english/listening-writings-and-vice-versa/.

[13] See p. 42.

add: "We are people with trajectories, not people with theories. In academia, you call cosmophobia a concept; I call it a germinating word."[14]

Those of us in academia – those of us who wrote this book in confluence with Bispo – are certainly not its protagonists. Rather, we are those who were affected by the world he carried. Nearly a century ago, Walter Benjamin introduced the concept of the "author as producer" to examine the role of artists during times of crisis. Today, perhaps we might speak of the role of the "writer as editor," understood here as an opportunity to address whatever doesn't fit within the solitary categories of author, writer, editor, or teacher. To put the oralization of writing first is to review positions of power and reverse epistemic roles in the face of the urgencies of our time. Yet if orality touches the materiality of printed letters, it does so only to return to orality once again. This approach follows the circular logic Bispo envisioned.

The function of this book is to provoke dialogue and conversation, to lead us from writing back to orality. It's in orality that words are alive. Beginning, middle, beginning.[15]

*

[14] Personal communication, May 2021.
[15] Personal communication, November 2022.

If we must transform Bispo's germinating words into "printed orality,"[16] and read them in this book, it is because we are incapable of listening to what the Earth tells us. We think the Earth belongs to us; we are cosmophobic. Literary mediation opens the way for the ancestral message to travel. In turn, *The Earth Gives, the Earth Wants* is the teachings of someone who listened to the Earth speak because he was inseparable from it. It is the Earth that teaches, cares, and warns.

Nêgo Bispo[17] was born in the Berlengas River Valley, Piauí, and lived in the Saco Curtume Quilombo until his passage into ancestry. This book is also an autobiography, but not in the sense we're used to. We must magnify the particle "bio" and weaken the prefix "auto" to perceive that in this auto-BIO-graphy, all lives are necessary. The key to life is necessarily collective. Life is only life if it is a cosmic dance.

In the opening lines of the book, Bispo is already inviting us to walk in the forest or fields with him: "the elders taught me to listen to the birdsongs and

[16] Marquez et al. (eds.), *Terra*.

[17] TR. "Nêgo Bispo" is the name under which Antônio Bispo dos Santos is publicly known and recognized in Brazil, particularly in the intellectual, cultural, and political debates with which his work engages. The notes to this text refer to Nêgo Bispo in keeping with this convention.

the whispers of the forest."[18] He and the Caatinga biome[19] are inseparable, indistinguishable in isolation. His auto-BIO-graphy calls on us not only to listen to the surroundings but, above all, to invert the usual composition of figure and ground. This book overturns the conventional rule that presents a figure (or character) against a background (or place), because it is also a territorial autobiography. The land converses with the *quilombo* and keeps Bispo company; he does not stand apart from the territory but coexists and speaks with it.

And when I speak of belonging to the quilombo, *I mean a relationship with the entire environment – with the animals and plants. We are only residents when we don't experience this belonging, when we are here but leave at the first chance we get.*[20]

Therefore, this book also calls on us to listen to the Earth and to address cosmophobia,[21] humanity's greatest illness. In cities, we almost never touch the Earth, and we almost never meet other-than-human beings. By modern definition and desire, cities are synthetic places that are paved, devitalized, and designed to

---

[18] See p. 19.
[19] TR. Caatinga biome: see p. 37, n. 8.
[20] See p. 51.
[21] TR. Cosmophobia: see p. 23, n. 4.

accommodate only humans (and only certain groups of humans, while others are excluded).

> *Humans have excluded all other possible forms of life in the city. Whatever other life tries to exist there is destroyed. If it does manage to exist, it's thanks to the power of the organic, not because humans want it there.*[22]

Yet Bispo shows that the strength of the organic is still present in the city. In what is also his territorial auto-biography, he tells us of his experiences and encounters in *favelas*, urban *quilombos*, and peripheral communities. These are his preferred urban spaces because of the vitality they sustain. The relationships with the land that emerge there – in the cracks of synthetic daily life – are for him the seeds of a counter-colonial future, even within cities.

> *The day the* quilombos *stop fearing the* favelas, *when the* favelas *trust the* quilombos, *and both join the villages in full confluence, the asphalt will melt!*[23]

*

We launched this book in Belo Horizonte at the Manzo Ngunzo Kaiango urban *quilombo* on the morning

---

[22] See p. 29.
[23] See p. 59. [TR. Asphalt and *favelas*: see p. 59, n. 14.]

of Saturday, May 20, 2023. We stood on *quilombola* territory that pre-dated the founding of that modern city in 1897. Though Manzo was recognized as part of the Cultural Heritage of Belo Horizonte in 2017 and of Minas Gerais in 2018, it continues to be a site of daily struggle and resistance. That morning, welcomed by the host Makota Kidoiale, a crowd gathered to listen to Bispo and to discover his new book.

The book's commercial success unsettled Bispo, who both wanted and did not want to see it published. I witnessed his dilemma before its publication. "*Quilombola* agriculture is not merchandise,"[24] he reflected. Yet a bestselling *quilombola* book, on the other hand, would perfectly fulfill the translator's mission that his community had entrusted him with decades earlier. At one point during our listening-writing process, I suggested the book's title, a phrase he often heard from his grandmother Mãe Joana: "The Earth gives, the Earth wants," she would say.

If I wrote above that the story of this book began in 2021, I must now amend this. I was naïve to suggest that linear time could define the beginning of this ancestral narrative process. How would it be possible to know the indomitable arrangements of circular time?

[24] Personal communication, March 2023.

How could we not publish a book whose title had been coined years earlier by my ancestor Mãe Joana?[25]

When I handed him the finished book, he looked at the paper object and asked, "Did the book really work? Because I haven't read it." I smiled. "Of course it worked, because you wrote it." That morning at the Manzo *quilombo*, Bispo concluded his reflections on the confluence of writing and resolved his dilemma about the book's publication. The book would be useful for both worlds.

Whoever reads this book will learn to speak. And I, who wrote it, will learn to read.

The following month, the book was launched at a fair in São Paulo. Bispo presented it to a large and attentive audience. At the end of his talk, an older Black man approached him and said, "I waited decades to hear what I heard today and to read a book like yours." Bispo realized that encounters like that one had already made the book's publication worth it.

When I bring the book into my university classes, something special always happens. Some students, often women, read the book and learn to speak. They

---

[25] Personal communication, May 2023.

learn to express themselves, share their stories, discuss the violent relationships they've had with their teachers and colleagues, and they work tirelessly to create a sense of belonging within the academic community. These are students who come from Brazil's urban peripheries, who bear family histories of exploitation, and who now occupy universities. They are tired of being "others" in the eyes of the academic white middle class. The book stirs up memories of their modes of knowledge production, trajectories that the university still fails to legitimize today. At such moments, this book opens up a return to orality.

Can we imagine other possibilities of being together? Will we be able to cultivate the abundance of existence instead of passively witnessing the catastrophe of the end? Bispo calls on us to find a place for confluences, where risky, necessary, and unforeseen arrangements may take root.

*

Seven months after that morning at Manzo, Bispo passed into ancestry. Shortly before leaving us, he had planned to be buried under a robust angico tree in the Saco Curtume Quilombo, his home in Piauí. Joana Maria, his daughter and guardian of his words, described how she was alarmed when, shortly after her father's funeral, the tree, native to the Caatinga biome, began to weaken until it withered completely. Joana was distressed and confused. She began to reflect on what the Earth was telling her.

From the soil around the dead tree, several shoots began to sprout. A community of small trees was born around the one that had died. Joana Maria's face lit up, and she smiled. "Dad is so clever!"

Nêgo Bispo's way of remaining present is through building a community of listeners and writers, readers and speakers, poets and landworkers, and practitioners in confluence dedicated to ensuring that life proliferates with strength, joy, beauty, and abundance. Even at the end of his life, when he was already unwell, and he seriously considered traveling less and restructuring the fields at Saco Curtume, the task that truly occupied him was sowing words and turning our minds into fields.

> *The time will come when people will have to come to the* quilombo *if they want to speak with me.*[26]

Ancestral knowledge never stops sprouting in the soil of the *quilombo*, among its human and non-human inhabitants. There, the counter-colonial world proliferates daily, organically, naturally, and incessantly. The

---

[26] Personal communication, March 2023.

quilombo's power is the heritage Bispo offers to the grandchildren-generation. Bispo generously invites us to partake in this heritage.

> *Our lives don't end. A grandmother-generation is the beginning, a mother-generation is the middle, and a grand-daughter-generation is the beginning again.*[27]

We are infinitely grateful for our confluence, Master Bispo.

Renata Marquez
September 2025

Translated by Alex Brostoff and Jamille Pinheiro Dias

[27] See p. 117. [TR. Generation terms: see p. 19, n. 2.]

Sowing Words

Smiling Wreath

In the early steps of my life, the elders taught me to listen to the birdsongs and the whispers of the forest. I think of the place where I first learned to walk as a kind of launchpad for my life's journey. One vivid memory from that time, still pulsing within me, is waking up to birdsong, an announcement of the day's weather.

The birds would tell us if it was going to rain, if the sun was going to shine, or if the skies were going to be overcast. Guided by their song, I already had a sense of what the day would bring before even getting out of bed. Another echo from my childhood is the walk to the *roça*,[1] a path we shared with older generations – our mother-generation and grandmother-generation.[2]

---

[1] TR. "*Roça*" refers to a plot of land cultivated using traditional methods, often involving slash-and-burn techniques. Typically used for subsistence farming, it is where staple crops such as manioc, corn, legumes, and tubers are grown. The term has been retained in Portuguese due to its cultural specificity, which has no exact equivalent in English.
[2] TR. "*Geração mãe*" (mother-generation) and "*geração avó*" (grandmother-generation) are neologisms in Portuguese, which we've echoed in English to convey the capaciousness of generational belonging to which Nêgo Bispo refers.

Along the way, we tuned into the sounds of the forest: the rustling of the wind, the flowing of streams, rivers, and waterfalls. Each echo was shaped by the terrain we crossed.

As we made our way to the *roça*, the birds kept singing, celebrating the abundance they had found while pecking in the fruit trees. Their songs also shared news of other beings nearby, sometimes as a warning about safety and protection, sometimes just to remind us that the surroundings were swelling with other presences. These are recurring memories, ones I return to whenever I face obstacles in my path. That's where I find renewal, and am propelled forward again, with more strength each time, able to overcome what lies ahead and keep going.

The memories of waking up in a house built from local materials also reverberate. Part of the roof was made from unvarnished adobe tiles, the other part was straw and wood. The room we slept in had adobe walls and tile roofing, perfect for the cool night air, making it the best place to rest.

Strangely enough, the kitchen was in the part of the house made of wattle-and-daub walls and a straw roof. Despite the fire hazard, that space was chosen precisely because straw and daub are thermal insulators. The kitchen stayed cooler during the day and held the wood-burning stove. Another room, with a straw roof and walls made of dry sticks, was where we gathered for communal activities like weaving. That space needed good ventilation, since weaving called for a steady breeze. Our architecture was in tune with the rhythms of the day; each room thoughtfully matched its purpose.

When I turned ten, I started training oxen. That's when I learned that training and colonizing are one and the same. Both the trainer and the colonizer begin by uprooting the being they seek to control, shattering its identity, stripping it from its cosmology, severing it from the sacred, imposing new ways of life on it, and giving it a different name. The act of naming is a way of erasing memory, so that another can be imposed on it.

There are trainers who use violence and trainers who use affection; trainers who punish and trainers who use food to create dependency – but they are all trainers. And all training has the same purpose: to make things work or produce objects of esteem and gratification. However, not all animals can be trained. Some become physically crippled when pushed harder than they are capable of going. Others become mentally stunted when subjected to violent mental shocks.

Similarly, there are people who are stunted: people who have not been conditioned to work, but who also can't manage to get by. People are conditioned so they can't imagine, so that they can't take care of themselves.

People who have not learned to do anything, or to take advantage of what's already been done. Stunted people who wander aimlessly, not knowing where to go. Or even people who have been conditioned and end up turning into a traveling working class, spending time in the South or Southeast in wage servitude, and then coming back up to the Northeast.

As for me, since I had mastered the art of training, I quickly understood that to face colonialist[3] society, there are times when "we must turn the weapons of our enemies into a means of defense," as one of my great masters used to say. So, to transform the art of naming into an art of defense, we decided to practice naming as well.

In other texts where I transcribed the ancestral knowledge of our grandmother-generation from orality into writing, we created certain names that people in academia call *concepts*. From there, we continued the practice of naming ways of being and of speaking as

---

[3] TR. Throughout this text, Nêgo Bispo speaks of colonization by using the adjective "colonialist." In Portuguese, this phrasing (e.g., "colonialist society") is less common than the more usual "colonial." We've echoed this choice in the English to name the modes of thinking, ideology, and institutions that reproduce and/or internalize colonization as a system. The choice is political, and part of what Nêgo Bispo will go on to describe as a "war of names." By naming the agents of colonialism directly (i.e., colonialists), he holds them accountable and makes responsibility visible.

a way to counter colonialism. This is what we call the *war of names*: the power-play of undermining colonial language through the act of renaming.

Once, a researcher from Cape Verde asked me, "How can we counter-colonize by speaking the enemy's language?" And I answered, "We will take the enemy's powerful words and weaken them. And we will take our own weakened words and empower them. For example, if the enemy loves to say *development*, we will say that development disconnects us, that development is a type of cosmophobia. We'll say that cosmophobia is a pandemic virus, and we will go after the word *development*. Because the better word is *involvement*."[4]

To weaken *sustainable development*, we used the word *biointeraction*; for *coincidence*, we used *confluence*; for

[4] TR. In the original Portuguese, Nêgo Bispo uses the term *"envolvimento"* ("involvement") in contrast to *"desenvolvimento"* ("development"). *"Envolvimento"* ("involvement") emphasizes a deeper engagement and connection with the Earth and other living beings. (On Earth/earth, see p. 29, n. 1.) For Nêgo Bispo, "development" is a term tied to cosmophobia, a fear of or disconnection from the cosmos and humanism, which seeks to position humans as creators separate from and superior to nature. The latter leads to a rupture in relationships with the Earth. *"Envolvimento"* ("involvement") represents a way of being that is organic, relational, and rooted in shared existence, rather than a linear process of progress or accumulation.

synthetic knowledge,[5] *organic* knowledge; for *transport*, *transfluence*; for *money* (or exchange), *sharing*; for *colonization, counter-colonization* . . . and so on. The researcher understood this word game: "You're right! Let's create more words in the Portuguese language, words that the Euro-colonizers themselves don't even have the courage to use!"

Why do people in the *favela*[6] use slang? They fill the Portuguese language with powerful words that the colonizer doesn't understand. They fill the language like they're stuffing a sausage. And so, they speak Portuguese in front of the enemy without him understanding. The *favela* has trained the language, enchanted it. We have to enchant the language. Can I say I'm a sorcerer? What's the problem? I'm both a sorcerer and a miracle worker, because I'm a polytheist and I know how to make things happen both by miracle and by spell.

I've sown the words *biointeraction, confluence, organic knowledge, synthetic knowledge, circular knowledge, linear knowledge, colonialism, counter-colonialism* . . .

---

[5] TR. Throughout the text, Nêgo Bispo uses the adjective "*sintético*" and the verb "*sintetizar*" to conceptualize how colonization has produced non-organic forms. Given their ongoing exploitative, extractivist, and other devastating impacts, not only commodities, but also cities, wind, fish, and even people are characterized as "synthetic" in what follows.

[6] TR. *Favela*: see p. 59, n. 14.

I've sown seeds that were ours and seeds that weren't. I've transformed our minds into *roças* and I've scattered a gourd of seeds. When I offered these seeds, these images, these germinating words, I had the impression that the word *biointeraction* would germinate more than others, and I put a lot of effort into that. But what happened was that the word that germinated best was *confluence*.

I have no doubt that *confluence* is the energy that moves us toward sharing, recognition, and respect. A river doesn't stop being a river when it joins another river; on the contrary, it becomes both itself and other rivers, it gains strength. When we enter into confluence, we don't stop being ourselves; we become ourselves and other selves – we make space. Confluence is a force that grows, that amplifies, that makes things flourish. That's the way. In fact, this germinating word, *confluence*, came to me at a time when our ancestors were holding me in their arms. In truth, they still hold me! I feel like I'm in the arms of ancestry and I want to share that.

Cities and Cosmophobia

What is a city? It's the opposite of a forest. The opposite of nature. The city is an artificial, *humanized* territory. The city is a territory designed exclusively for humans. Humans have excluded all other possible forms of life in the city. Whatever other life tries to exist there is destroyed. If it does manage to exist, it's thanks to the power of the organic, not because humans want it there.

I grew up in a house with a dirt floor, where I went barefoot. The chickens and the other animals lived with us in the house. Whenever there were chicken droppings on the dirt floor, the damp part would be absorbed into the earth.[1] We'd throw the solid part away in the yard to serve as fertilizer. For city folks, this is horrifying. Stepping on chicken droppings? Absolutely not! You've got to have a well-tiled floor so that you can see other

---

[1] TR. The Portuguese word "*terra*" can mean earth, land, or soil. Throughout this translation, the distinction between "earth" as soil/ground is marked through as lowercase, whereas the capitalized "Earth" refers to the subject/agentive being. In this sentence, for example, the earth refers specifically to the material ground rather than the planetary being.

life forms, and any other living thing that might be there, get rid of it; disinfect all the micro-organisms. Kill even what you can't see. To be barefoot, the floor has to be disinfected: tiles were created because humans can't step on the earth. Shoes were created because humans can't step on the earth. Because the earth is our original source of longing.

Original sin drove a wedge between humanity and nature. Our punishment was being expelled from nature. This is why Adam was expelled from the Garden of Eden and humanism became a system; a realm disconnected from the animal kingdom. All plants fit in the plant kingdom; all minerals fit in the mineral kingdom. But humans don't fit in the animal kingdom. Humans don't see themselves as part of the animal world. This disconnection is an effect of cosmophobia.

Cosmophobia is fear, an illness that doesn't have a cure; it's only resisted through immunity. And what immunization could protect us from cosmophobia? Counter-colonization. In other words, polytheism, because cosmophobia germinates in monotheism. If we abandon monotheism and embrace polytheism, we'll be immunized. In the polytheistic world, original sin doesn't exist; no one was expelled from the Garden of Eden, no one remembers the terror. There are many gods and goddesses, and we aren't afraid to speak to them. In the polytheistic world, no one fights over one God, because there are many gods and goddesses – enough for everyone. In the monotheistic world, there's only one God; there's constant conflict. Israelis against Palestinians, for example. People are being killed over the fight for God. In our case, this is unnecessary. We have Exu, Tranca Rua, Pomba Gira, Maria Padilha[2] … If we're not with one, we're with another.

When I left at eighteen and went to a city, I realized another world existed beyond the one where I was born and grew up. The city was a different world. In the cities, people didn't know how to build their own homes like we did where I came from. People from the city didn't know how, so they depended on others to do it for them. Where I was born and raised, everyone had a house. Only people who didn't want a house didn't have one, and then they lived with their parents, extended family, or friends. Or there were those who wandered, who thought it was good not to have a house because it was a lot of work to maintain one. But it wasn't like that in the city. People depended on houses they didn't know how to build. Where I was born and raised, from childhood, we would go out exploring, find a spot we liked, and form a connection with it, a means of communication with the place. And we would

[2] TR. Spiritual figures from Afro-Brazilian religions.

say, "I'm going to build my house here." I didn't need to pay anyone to build my house. On the contrary, on construction days, everyone came together. It was a big collective effort, a celebration, and we'd build a house very quickly.

When I got to the city, I realized that to build a house, it was necessary to pay: to pay for land, pay for everything. When knowledge is transformed into a commodity and hierarchized, what measure justifies a bricklayer's apprentice earning less than a bricklayer? Or an engineer earning more than a bricklayer if the engineer only knows how to draw and no one lives inside those drawings? If the bricklayer is the person who builds the house and lives in the house he built, the engineer shouldn't get anything. The engineer shouldn't be paid; the bricklayer should. For us, engineering is unnecessary. It only exists within the logic of a monotheistic, Euro-Christian society.

I stayed in the big city for about five years, until the moment I realized that it wasn't where I belonged. I couldn't live in the big city, and I returned to the country to live in the *roça* where I still am today. The city didn't fit me. While society is built by proprietors, our communities are built by people. In the city, people were afraid of one another. In our communities, no one was afraid of anyone. We lived in peace. There was no stealing or robbing in our communities. If a person was passing by my *roça* and grabbed a piece of fruit to eat, it made me happy; it was a mode of recognition, as if I had received a trophy.

City people feel the need to accumulate: to accumulate money, to accumulate things. They are disconnected from nature. They don't feel like nature. Cities are colonialist structures. Not all city people are colonialists, but cities are colonialist territories. There are people struggling to survive in this colonialist territory. When I speak of city folk, I speak of Euro-Christian colonialists, but from a territorial perspective.

Adults from the city would pretend to do things and other adults would pay to watch them: it was what they called theater. When art turns into a commodity, it becomes a game of not doing anything. Theater is about doing things as play, while in our community, play is about really doing things. When we pretend to be performing the Reisado,[3] we're actually doing the Reisado. When we pretend to be working in the *roça*, we're growing up learning how to hoe the land. We

---

[3] TR. A festive Brazilian folk tradition that blends music, dance, and drama. This celebration – rooted in both Catholic devotion and local cultural practices – narrates the journey of the Three Kings to visit the newborn Jesus. Performed by groups known as "Reisado troupes," the event incorporates characters drawn from colonial history and regional folklore, animated through rhythmic dances set to percussion.

pretend until we actually know how to plant, until we make a real *roça*. We pretend to do things, and we do things, while theater people pretend to do nothing, or do pretend things, and so don't do anything real at all.

Theater, like any other type of commercialized art, prevents conversation between souls, because art is a conversation between souls. Art feeds life: it shouldn't be a commodity. No one knows who composed the Congado[4] songs; there isn't a patent. Anyone can sing them. Anyone can play the Congado snare drums in the rhythms and melodies that were composed.

We don't know the composer of most of the songs sung in the *quilombo*.[5] One of our artists once explained how they didn't write to sell. "I write so people sing. If you want to sing, sing! Here's the music. Why do you need to buy a song to sing if everyone is already singing? Sing the song, man!"

Art is a conversation between souls because it travels from the individual to the collective, so it's shared. Culture is the opposite. We don't have culture, we have

[4] TR. An Afro-Brazilian cultural and religious celebration that reenacts the coronation of the King of Congo. Blending Catholic and African traditions, Congado features music, dance, colorful costumes, and processions.

[5] TR. *Quilombos* are Afro-Brazilian settlements established by maroon communities of formerly enslaved people; their cultural and religious traditions have been maintained across centuries.

ways: ways of seeing, of feeling, of doing things, ways of life. And these ways can be changed. When a ritual takes place in the *terreiro*[6] and someone begins a song, everyone sings along. One person starts the chant – it's shared, and soon everyone is singing the words. That's how we do it. In cultural practice, you must follow the notes. Culture is a standardized, commodified, colonial thing. Colonialists say we don't have culture when we don't act like them. Someone who doesn't know how to play the piano or doesn't know what classical music is, who's never been to a theater, who never goes to the movie theater – for them, that person has no culture. For us, someone who doesn't know how to sing and dance to the rhythm of percussion, someone who doesn't know how to cook a dish, who isn't moved by birdsong, doesn't have a pleasant life.

While people from the city felt very important, I, in turn, felt necessary. They, however, didn't see me as someone necessary; they saw me as someone useful. For them, I was a server, a servant. I was useful, but

---

[6] TR. A sacred communal space used for Afro-Brazilian religious and cultural practices, particularly in Umbanda and Candomblé (see also p. 62, nn. 15 and 16, respectively, for these traditions). A *terreiro* serves as both a spiritual center and a place of gathering, where rituals, ceremonies, music, dance, and healing take place. It often functions as a key site of cultural transmission and resistance in Afro-Brazilian communities.

I could be replaced because I wasn't necessary. That's when I understood that city people form relationships based on usefulness and importance, not on necessity. For us, someone who is "important" means almost nothing. It's that person who thinks they're great but doesn't serve others. For us, "necessary" is the term that carries real value. There are people who are "necessary" and there are people who are "important." People who are important think that other people are there to serve them. Necessary people are different. They're people whose presence we seek out. People whose presence is needed; people we follow.

In the city, there were only schools for reading and writing. There weren't any other kinds of schools, schools for inspiration or play. When the government schools for reading and writing reached our territory, it happened very quickly. Writing forced its way in, determined at any cost to become the dominant language. We were confronted with a major challenge: our contracts, which had always been made orally, were suddenly attacked and forced into written form.

This education system considered our keepers of the oral tradition unnecessary, and tried to replace them with writing teachers. At that moment, after spending so much time playing, I had to go to this kind of school to learn what was happening in another world through writing: the world of written words, the world beyond the community. I went to the school for reading and writing to be necessary, not to be important. To be able to help our community find solutions.

In the *quilombo*, we tell stories by moonlight, at the full moon, around the fire. The stories are told in a way that's enjoyable and for everyone. In big cities, however, only what can be sold is valuable. They don't tell stories there; stories are just written. Writing stories is a profession. We tell stories without charging anyone anything. We do it to strengthen our paths forward. And we don't just tell stories about human beings. We also tell stories about animals: monkeys, jaguars, and little birds.

The *codorniz*[7] is a Caatinga[8] bird. It's like a quail. When we were kids, we set traps to catch them. The *codorniz* would fall into the trap, but when we got close, it would faint. It would play dead under the trap. "How did it die? Was there a snake?" we'd think. And, of course, you can't eat a bird when you don't know how it died. Since we would need to empty the trap,

---

[7] TR. A small ground-dwelling bird from the Caatinga biome (see n. 8 below), similar to a quail, that is traditionally hunted in north-eastern Brazil.

[8] TR. Caatinga is a biome found primarily in Brazil's Northeast and parts of northern Minas Gerais. Characterized by a hot, semi-arid climate, it features shallow, rocky soils and resilient, scrubland vegetation. The landscape includes low-growing trees and shrubs with thick trunks and deep roots, adapted to long dry seasons and scarce rainfall.

we would take the "dead" *codorniz* out and put it aside. And suddenly, it would fly away! The *codorniz* hadn't died at all. It was a trick! The *codorniz* taught us how to hide, how to disguise ourselves. In cities, soap operas and theaters are where people play dead.

Where I was born and grew up, we had an organic relationship with all forms of life. All lives are necessary, not important. We would chase a pig to catch it and put it in the sty. We would pretend to be running to get somewhere, by necessity. In cities, it's different: I see people running without knowing where they're going, without knowing why they're running – just because a doctor said they have to run! I also ran in the city without knowing where or why I was running. Why don't people from cities interact with nature? Because they're afraid. Because they're cosmophobic.

We only fish in the river when it's necessary because we trust the river. We're not afraid of the river. We know that the river will always provide fish. Why do we only collect fruit when it's necessary? Because we know that we'll always have fruit. When it's not good fruit, there'll be more. When there's no *umbu*,[9] there'll be *juá*,[10] there'll

[9] TR. *Umbu* is a native fruit tree of Brazil's semi-arid Northeast (*Spondias tuberosa*).

[10] TR. *Juá* (or *joazeiro*) refers to a tree native to Brazil, whose small fruits are edible and often used in traditional medicinal practices.

be *carnaúba*.[11] When there's no *carnaúba*, there'll be *caruá*.[12]

When there's no *caruá*, there'll be *grão de galo*,[13] there'll be *quipá*,[14] there'll be *macambira*,[15] there'll be *xique*,[16] there'll be *mandacaru*.[17] They're offerings from the Caatinga that feed humans and non-humans. There are things in the Caatinga that humans don't consume. But non-humans eat them and then share them with us. Since we know there's enough for everyone, we're not

[11] TR. A palm tree native to northeastern Brazil (*Copernicia prunifera*), known for its wide range of uses, especially its wax, which is extracted from its leaves.

[12] TR. A spiky-leafed plant from the pineapple family (*Bromeliacea*), found in Brazil's drylands, traditionally used for fiber extraction and sometimes for its small fruits.

[13] TR. A common name for various small-seeded plants of the *Cordia* genus, particularly within the borage family (*Boraginaceae*), native to Brazil. The literal translation is "rooster's grain."

[14] TR. A cactus species native to northeastern Brazil (*Tacinga inamoena*), recognized for its spiny pads and edible fruits traditionally consumed in rural communities.

[15] TR. A tropical plant from the pineapple family (*Bromeliaceae*), native to Brazil's semi-arid regions and valued for its resistance to drought and for its fibrous leaves.

[16] TR. A type of cactus native to Brazil's Caatinga biome (*Pilosocereus gounellei*), known for its ability to thrive in arid conditions and often used as forage during droughts.

[17] TR. A tall, columnar cactus (*Cereus jamacaru*) native to Brazil's semi-arid regions, recognized by its large white flowers and symbolic presence in northeastern folklore.

afraid, and we don't need to stockpile. Only those who don't have any sense of trust need to stockpile, those who fear that nature won't provide for them, who fear nature might punish them.

Cosmophobia is responsible for this cruel system of stockpiling, of disconnectedness, of expropriation, and of unnecessary extraction. Cosmophobia is also responsible for trash. Why is there so much trash? Because people accumulate more than is necessary and time passes. They need a certain amount of fruit, but they buy more than they need. Wastefulness is a result of cosmophobia. Cosmophobia is necessary for development; it's about disconnection, about moving away from where we come from. Cosmophobia is the same as original sin. And everything that's original scares monotheistic Euro-Christians.

One of my grandmothers and teachers used to teach us that whatever we don't need but know will rot should be thrown in the *quintal*.[18] And whatever isn't necessary but doesn't rot should be kept until it is necessary. This way, nothing goes into the trash. We didn't know the

[18] In many Brazilian households, a *quintal* refers to a multifunctional outdoor area adjoining the home. Often unpaved, this space serves a variety of domestic purposes, including hanging laundry, raising poultry, preparing food, growing herbs or fruit trees, and hosting family gatherings. It is both a utilitarian and social space, often central to daily life.

word "trash." Sometimes I'd ask, "What do I do with this?" My grandmother would ask, "Does it rot? If it rots, throw it in the brush." Throwing something in the brush meant throwing it into the woods, because it would decompose and become necessary for other lives. But when I got to the city and said, "Look, this is no good, it's not necessary anymore, I'm going to throw it in the brush," people teased me. In the city, there was no brush; there was trash. And everything is thrown in the trash: things that rot and things that don't. Everything mixed.

I lived in São Cristóvão, in Rio de Janeiro, and every weekend and in all my free time I went to Quinta da Boa Vista. I never loved Copacabana. For me, Copacabana is a plastic thing, a disposable toy. For me, the synthetic part of Rio feels disposable. When I go to Rio de Janeiro now, I go to the Maré *favela*, to the Complexo do Alemão, to the Pereirão *favela*, and I feel good. I'm warmly welcomed in each of them. And I feel good there – where it smells like people, where there are things that are still organic, and where the language is alive and continually being adapted. Maré always has a spot for me to stay, to cook corn with beans, to chat and have a drink. The same happens in Pereirão, in Santa Teresa.

One way of dealing with money is just to spend it, to use it up so it won't make our lives miserable. Another way is to boycott it. When I travel, I don't spend money on hotels, and instead of going to a shopping mall, I go to the street markets, because in the markets I see people who look like me, who sweat, who are organic. People in shopping malls don't sweat. At malls, there's no smell of sweat, only synthetic smells, the smells of abstract products.[19]

While society is made up of equals, a community is made up of diverse beings. We are diversal[20] beings; we are cosmological, natural, and organic. We're not humanists. Humanists are people who transform nature into money, into cars of the year. We're all of the cosmos, except for humans. I'm not human. I am *quilombola*. I'm a landworker, a fisherman, a being of the cosmos. Humans are the monotheistic Euro-Christians. They're afraid of the cosmos. Cosmophobia is humanity's worst disease.

Despite being creatures of nature, humanists detach themselves from nature and turn into creators. That's

[19] TR. "Abstract products," which also sounds unusual in the Portuguese, refers to that which is artificial, commodified, and/or disconnected from organic life in relation to the Earth. They are symptoms of the colonialist and cosmophobic mindset Nêgo Bispo critiques.

[20] TR. "Diversal" (a neologism in Brazilian Portuguese) names a plurality grounded in confluence rather than universalism. The term belongs to Nêgo Bispo's "war of names," a counter-colonial lexicon opposing cosmophobia and extractive "development."

why they need to make the organic synthetic, to call all life "raw material." This raw material becomes an object to be improved, monetized, and synthesized by humans. They feel like the owners of intelligence, gods even – the gods of vertical logic, of power, of interference in the lives of others, of manipulation. Not gods of biointeraction.

Humanism walks hand in hand with the word *development*, an idea of treating humans like beings who want to be creators, who want to overcome nature, rather than creatures of nature. On the opposite side of the humanists are the *diversal beings* – the cosmological or organic beings. If humans always want to transform the organic into the synthetic, as diversal beings, we just want to live organically, becoming increasingly organic. For diversal beings, it's not about developing, but involving. While we engage organically, they want to develop humanistically.

Humanity is against involvement, it's against living engaged with the trees, with the land, with the woods. Development is synonymous with disconnection. It pulls us out of the cosmos. For Euro-Christians, to bind oneself to the cosmos is a sin. They try to humanize and make everything that's original into something synthetic.

This isn't binary thinking, but border thinking. We'll never cross over to humanism's side, but we'll also never want humanism to cross over to our side. We also don't want humanism to stop existing; we just want there to be respect and border dialogues. Humanity is there; we're not going to erase it. But how are we going to relate to humanity? By establishing borders. It could be that in the future, since borders are shifting, elastic territories, we'll advance and they'll retreat, or we'll retreat and they'll advance, but without reaching the limit. We always think circularly, breaking monism, duality, and binarism.

Humanists want to convince us that globalization is an expansive coexistence when in fact it's not. Instead of understanding the globe as a diversal form with various ecosystems, various languages, various species, and various kingdoms, when the humanists speak of "globalizing," they're talking about "unifying." They're saying one currency, one language, few minds. For humans, there is no globalization. For them, what exists is the history of Eurocentrism – of centrality, of oneness. What they call globalization is universality. Not in the sense that we understand universality, but in the sense of oneness.

Pat Roy Mooney's "The ETC Century"[21] brings up an important fact: the proportion of the four most

---

[21] TR. Pat Roy Mooney, "The ETC Century: Erosion, Technological Transformation and Corporate Concentration in the 21st Century," *Development Dialogue*, 1–2 (1999).

translated languages in the world (English, Spanish, French, and German) grew from 65% to 1980 to 81% in 1994. Humans don't want to globalize in the sense of the diversal, but in the sense of unifying, of trans- forming everything into one thing. When they talk about the individual, they talk about uniqueness. When we ourselves talk about the individual, we're talking about unity. We're saying "one," but this "one" is part of everything, of the universe. If for the humanists the "one" is the universe, for us, there's only "one" because there's more than one. We see a difference between being "one" and being singular, while for the humanists, the "one" and the singular are the same thing. When we say "globe," we're simultaneously encompassing and recognizing the individualities around the globe. This is a germinating matter, which needs to be raised and cultivated.

We are Sharers

When I hear the word *confluence* or the word *sharing* out in the world, I feel festive. But when I hear *exchange*, I always say, "Careful, it's not an exchange, it's sharing." Because *exchange* means a watch for a watch, one object for another object, whereas *sharing* means one action for another action, one gesture for another gesture, affection for affection. And affection isn't exchanged, it's shared.

When I feel affection for someone, I receive the same in return. Affection flows back and forth. Sharing is something that yields and multiplies.

When I got to the territory where I live today, there were already other sharers who welcomed us. In the Caatinga, the *umbu* trees received us. They shared their fruit, their leaves, and their roots with us when we arrived, and we didn't bring anything for the *umbu* trees. They were already native here. We came to dwell in this land after them. It was the same with the birds. It was the same with a plant called *pinhão*[1] – not the edible kind,

[1] TR. This refers to *pinhão-bravo* (*Jatropha mollissima*), a Caatinga plant whose seeds are eaten by doves such as the *juriti*, distinct from the edible *Araucaria* pine seeds of southern Brazil.

but a *pinhão* we humans cared for, and which was dearly loved by the *juriti*[2] doves. They eat these seeds, and from time to time, we catch a *juriti*. The *pinhão* shares with the *juriti*, the *juriti* shares with us, and we again share with the *pinhão*. Now that we've been here longer, we, too, have come to be part of the local cycle of sharing.

If I see a tree that's not doing well, I'll care for it, and it will benefit both me and other beings. There is a tree in the Caatinga called *jacurutu*. The *jacurutu* is a thorny, lush tree that gets very large. It has medicinal properties but doesn't bear fruit for us. Still, it provides shade for everyone, all year round, which is its way of sharing. When we need blessed shade to ease the heat of the sun, the *jacurutu* shelters us. For us, a *jacurutu* tree is like a canopy for someone living in the city.

Sometimes you're walking and find a beautiful, comfortable stone to sit on. Or a flat rock where you can lie down and rest. This kind of sharing is so abundant, so present in our lives, that we rarely even mention it to people in the city. If you're walking and see a rat running through the woods, there's a chance that a snake is just behind it. The rat is sharing a warning: "Don't walk here now. It might not be safe." A rat in the forest isn't as bad as a rat in the city. A forest rat is a sharer. If I see food that

---

[2] TR. A *juriti* is a common Brazilian dove (*Leptotila spp.*), known for its soft call.

serves the rat, I'll have to leave it there, because the rat might be an informant. The *cancã*[3] is a bird that always warns us about snakes. If I'm in the Caatinga and hear a *cancã* singing, I know there's something I need to pay attention to – maybe a snake, or a tegu lizard.[4] Sometimes it's something harmless, but the *cancã* leaves a signal.

Once we start living in a new place, we gradually become sharers. In the *quilombo*, we are sharers if we were born there or if we belong to it. And when I speak of belonging to the *quilombo*, I mean a relationship with the entire environment – with the animals and plants. We are only residents when we don't experience this belonging, when we are here but leave at the first chance we get.

I was born and raised at the crossroads of biomes, where the semi-arid region, the coconut palm groves, the pre-Amazon, and now and then some signs of what's called the Atlantic Forest meet. When I was born, that territory was home to and occupied by Afro-confluent[5]

---

[3] TR. White-naped jay.

[4] TR. The tegu is a large lizard native to South America, typically reaching around one meter in length. It is known for its striking coloration and adaptability to different environments, often found in forests, savannas, and even agricultural areas.

[5] TR. Nêgo Bispo uses the term "Afro-confluent" rather than "Afro-descendant" to highlight the ongoing presence of African and *quilombola* ways of living. For him, confluence suggests a relational, non-linear ontology where identities are constantly (re)shaped through experience, oral tradition, and their connection to land.

people. Most of them were my relatives. The other families were also Afro-confluent. There were more than eighteen wooden mills powered by animals for making *rapadura* sugar that belonged to Afro-confluent people. There is no evidence that the people of that territory were ever enslaved.

We don't have a memory of our grandmother-, great-grandmother-, or great-great-grandmother-generations being enslaved. My great-uncle was born in the nineteenth century. That means my great-grandfather was born before the *Lei Áurea*,[6] and my great-great-grandfather was born long before that. We've never heard of enslavement in our family. And we've never had bosses.

Our relationships with non-Afro-confluent and non-Indigenous people in that territory were based on respect and shared power. And when there was any imbalance, it actually worked in our favor, because we held a vast confluence of knowledge. We knew everything needed to live well in that environment. Our family grew what it needed, was masterful in agriculture, and knew how to process everything. We made the equipment used to process cassava, sugarcane,

---

[6] TR. In 1888, Brazil formally abolished slavery through a decree signed by Princess Isabel. This historic act, known as the *Lei Áurea* or "Golden Law," marked the official end of over three centuries of enslavement in the country.

and alcohol. A people who knew all that were likely never enslaved and never had their memory erased the way the Euro-Christian colonialists intended and still intend to today.

I was raised playing – pretending to do what the elders did. They spent their days at the mill making *rapadura* sugar, molasses, and other products derived from sugarcane, processing it with animal-powered machinery. As children, we would do the same, but as a game. We pretended to make flour and grind sugarcane, building little mills and pretending to produce things, except our oxen weren't real; they were handcrafted. We used what we had around us; we carved *mandacaru* wood. We pretended to be adults; we did what the adults did. That's how we learned. But we also played during festivals – celebrations born of our people's arts, our people's culture.

In our communities, there were people who made musical instruments and others who played them. Some did both, and others sang. At parties, everyone took turns. These parties weren't commodities. My grandmother used to say there was the *festa* and there was the *furdunço*. The *festa* was a celebration, a joyful gathering, a true festivity. The *furdunço* made a bit of a racket – a noisy scene created just to make money, with no connection to life, with no authenticity. If there was no real reason to celebrate, she'd call it *furdunço*.

Money didn't circulate in our environment. The community was made up of large families, and all of them grew sugarcane. You needed many hands for milling. When a single family wasn't enough, what did we do? If I grew sugarcane and ten of my friends grew sugarcane, we would join each other. One week we'd help one person, the next week another, and so on. No one stockpiled the product because while you were milling, I'd take what I needed from your mill. And when it was my turn, you'd take what you needed from mine. That's how we spent the dry season. Only during the final millings would anyone store things for the rainy season, when the milling stopped. It was a vast act of sharing. No one spoke of money. There was abundance.

There were all sorts of pranks. Sometimes folks would sneak in and take chickens from a neighbor without being seen. It was a skill. It was cool to see who had a knack for the art of pilfering. My father, who was quite the trickster, once made a bet with three cousins to see who could steal a watermelon from their grandfather's *roça* without him noticing. Everyone could recognize each other's tracks and habits. If someone went into the *roça*, our grandfather would know who it was for sure. He was very sharp, so they concluded the only way to steal from him was right in front of him – that was the only time he wouldn't be suspicious. Our grandfather was working when the four of them arrived, but one cousin stayed outside the *roça*. Two of the others distracted our grandfather with a conversation while the third grabbed a watermelon and passed it to the person waiting outside. They only needed one watermelon to be proof of the feat, like a trophy.

The cousin who took the watermelon went to a nearby waterfall, the meeting spot. The others, once they saw our grandfather was fully distracted, ran off toward the waterfall, celebrating. But when they got there, the cousin had already eaten the watermelon with some other friends. They had robbed our grandfather, but the cousin had robbed *them*! He was the smartest and most cunning of them all.

Those pranks were part of their training in self-defense, because one day it might be needed during colonialist attacks. It would come in handy if the colonialists ever showed up, like when the Prestes Column[7] passed through.

We also trained in self-defense at the sugar mills. *Jucá*[8] was one of our most beautiful forms of defense. At the end

[7] TR. A major political and military campaign that took place from 1924 to 1927, spanning from southern to northern Brazil. Composed largely of poor rural workers, the movement called for greater social justice.
[8] TR. *Jucá* is an Afro-Brazilian martial art developed in *quilombo* communities, practiced using a club carved from the hardwood of the *jucá* tree.

of the workday, we would train with people from other mills. We practiced *jucá*, knife games, and other kinds of defense. The mill wasn't just a mill. A *rapadura* mill was everything you could use in sugarcane processing to support daily life. *Rapadura* was also used to feed the animals. The cane straw was used as food too. While working at the mill, we also got firewood, fencing materials, and shade, because in the Caatinga, it gets cold during the rainy season, but during the dry season, it's extremely hot.

In the rainy season, we worked on the *roça*. But during the dry season, we went to the flour houses and the mills, where we could work in the shade. We spent two months in the shade, celebrating. You didn't earn money at the flour houses or at the mills. You earned flour, tapioca, dough, and *crueira*.[9]

People who hadn't planted sugarcane but knew how to do something useful would work in exchange for *rapadura*,[10] honey, vinegar, sugar, or *cachaça*.[11] Those who didn't have a mill would go on to get what they needed. Everyone had a way to get supplies.

---

[9] TR. A coarse byproduct of cassava processing, consisting of fibrous fragments left over after the starch is extracted. In many rural Brazilian communities, *crueira* is used as an ingredient in cooking, particularly in traditional dishes prepared during cassava flour production.

[10] TR. Raw sugarcane.

[11] TR. Sugarcane liquor.

The cities are in the *quilombos*. It's not the *quilombos* that are in Belo Horizonte. Belo Horizonte is located within the Souza, Manzo, and Luízes *quilombos*, for example. Some of our Afro-confluent people's most significant counter-colonial expressions are in the *quilombos* where the state of Minas Gerais is located. Many *quilombola* practices and their organic knowledge systems have been preserved there – our ways of seeing, doing, feeling, and living. In many other *quilombos* located in other states, these practices have been destroyed by the State. Perhaps the word isn't *destroyed*, but made precarious.

Here in the *quilombos* where the state of Piauí is, *beiju*[12] was once one of the most loved breakfast foods, along with tapioca cakes. But these foods have been devalued due to underrepresentation, ridicule by colonialist perspectives, and State intervention through public health agencies. I live five kilometers from the school where my granddaughter and grandsons study, but I'm not allowed to sell the goats we raise for school meals because the town doesn't have an adequate sanitary inspection system to test and certify the quality of the food. How can the same meat that my grandchildren eat at my house every day not be

---

[12] TR. A type of tapioca pancake made from cassava starch.

considered safe for them to eat at school? That doesn't make any sense.

In the *quilombos* where Minas Gerais is, we see that many traditional foods are still preserved, and the public health authorities haven't had the power to eliminate them. There's a stronger structure in place there, especially because of the festivals. Any food practice that is connected to a celebration becomes stronger. When food traditions become disconnected or displaced from the festivals, they're weakened.

Congado is a form of resistance against colonialists, and it has the power to sustain an entire part of a culture, including cuisine, appreciation, and the food experience that forms part of the celebration. Without that food, the celebration can't happen. The celebration preserves the food and the food preserves the celebration. This is true in the *terreiros* and many other festive traditions. In the case of Piauí, the *batuques*[13] and the foods prepared for them have endured: our celebrations defend our food practices, because the festival is stronger than the Law. The State can't break down ways of life when they are woven into celebration.

There's no celebration without food, and no food without celebration, just as there's no food without

[13] TR. Afro-Brazilian festivities that feature percussion, singing, and dancing.

planting. The traditional dishes associated with each celebration follow from a shared way of life and the growing cycle. During festival time, even those who don't plant have access to the harvest. Food nourishes the body and the soul. For us, food isn't just food. The beans from the supermarket brought to our celebrations become something else entirely; they take on other lives, other spirits. They're no longer the same beans – they become something else.

We didn't create the *quilombos* alone. To form *quilombos*, we had to bring knowledge from Africa with us, but the Indigenous peoples here told us that what worked one way there worked differently here. It was in this confluence of knowledge that the *quilombos* were formed, invented by Afro-confluent peoples in dialogue with Indigenous peoples. The day the *quilombos* stop fearing the *favelas*, when the *favelas* trust the *quilombos*, and both join the villages in full confluence, the asphalt will melt![14]

The *quilombo* territories where cities now sit are places where there should be markets, but not like

---

[14] TR. In the urban landscape of cities such as Rio de Janeiro, a common social distinction is drawn between the so-called *asfalto* (literally "asphalt") and the *favelas*. *Asfalto* neighborhoods have paved roads and formal infrastructure, generally associated with middle- and upper-class residents. *Favelas*, which are also called *morros* when located on hillsides, are informal settlements historically associated with working-class and marginalized populations.

shops where you buy something and leave. Markets like the ones in the Caatinga or the Sertão, where most people arrive early in the morning and don't leave until the end of the day. There are those who buy, those who sell, those who lend, those who trade, and those who come just to hear the latest news, meet friends, and have a *cachaça*. Every proper market must also have a little *cabaré* – a space for a bohemian lifestyle, for flirting, for romance and dance. The people who go to the *cabarés* dance very well; they're the places where people learn how to dance and flirt, places for affection.

For spaces like this to exist, *favelas* need new means of self-organization. In a market held in a *favela*, people could come together to talk about the police, to coordinate and strategize, to build and share their systems of defense. *Favelas* need to pirate technologies, build their own underground bicycle factories. They build them, the police come and confiscate them, and then they build them again. It's time to stir things up, to steal and break the patents! *Favelas* need to have their own products, and China is a major inspiration. We wouldn't have cellphones today if the Chinese hadn't ignored the cellphone patents. I wouldn't be able to communicate today; I do so thanks to piracy. The *favela* needs to specialize in pirating everything it possibly can, using the technology and wisdom of our people.

There are ways of life outside of colonization, but not politics. All politics is a colonial instrument, because politics is about managing other people's lives. Politics is not self-governance. Politics is produced by a group that sees itself as enlightened and therefore entitled to be the protagonist in others' lives. Democracy is an inherently human concept. Other beings – other living things in the world – don't engage in this system. Their lives don't look anything like that. Cattle, pigs, chickens, birds – none of them have this kind of management structure. Their form of governance is something else entirely. Only humans have this system where one person lives to manage another's life in a top-down fashion, while claiming to defend others' rights. Among other living beings, each being defends itself in a partial way to protect the territory as a whole.

One person nevertheless wants to govern 200 million other people. How could they if they don't even know two thousand other people? How do you govern people you don't know? In the animal kingdom, politics exists only among humans. In other species, there is self-governance. There's no group of goats trying to govern all the other herds. Each group of goats forms its own herd. Each group of pigs forms its own group. Animals live in herds, clusters within the same species. Not all peccaries want to live in the same sounder; there are multiple sounders of peccaries.

When a beehive gets too large, a queen leaves to form a new hive. When a wasp nest gets too crowded, they build a new one. When an anthill gets too big, the ants make another. Why haven't we learned that in self-governance, the group must be just the right size to govern itself? An Umbanda[15] or Candomblé[16] temple doesn't want to host the whole world; it doesn't want the entire city to attend. It only wants a portion of the people. And when it gets too large, another temple is founded. They only want to host numbers they can truly welcome.

At the beginning of the COVID-19 pandemic, some parts of society sounded the alarm: "The *quilombolas* will die, the Indigenous people will die; they'll be the first to die because they're the most vulnerable." Parts of society invented this idea that we're the most vulnerable. I live in a *quilombo* with over a hundred families, and we're just five kilometers from the city. *Quilombos* don't have an overcrowding issue. We live at a distance from each other; we visit each other, but not in large numbers. We go to the *roça* every day.

---

[15] TR. Umbanda is an Afro-Brazilian religion that blends elements of African traditions, Catholicism, Spiritism, and Indigenous practices.

[16] TR. Candomblé is an Afro-Brazilian religion centered on the worship of Orixás (deities) through rituals involving music, dance, and offerings.

Out there, it's just us and the forest. Here, we practice self-governance.

We have a community association, but it only exists so we can deal with the State, which is why no one's really interested in being president. Our form of governance is enacted by the collective: at funerals, at parties, birthdays, masses, in the *terreiros*, in the *roças*. If a problem comes up, we solve it right then and there. Meanwhile, the politicians gather in Brasília to solve the pandemic in the Amazon. And while they're talking, people are dying without oxygen because the ones making decisions are in Brasília.

Politics is Euro-Christian and monotheistic, and even cosmopolitics is a Euro-Christian invention. But we *quilombolas* don't have politics; we have ways of life. We don't hold formal meetings to solve our issues. We have discussions – sometimes heated – where we argue until we reach an understanding. Then we drink *cachaça* to celebrate.

Our movement is one of transfluence. Through transfluence, we are beginning, middle, and beginning again. Because we transflow, conflow, and transflow. We conflow, transflow, and conflow again. The order doesn't matter.

For us, content determines form, and form determines content. If I go looking for a shoe that fits my foot, then my foot is the form, and the shoe is the content. It's the shoe that has to fit the shape of my foot. But if, like the colonialists, those synthetic peoples, I go looking for a foot to fit a shoe – if I have a shoe in search of a foot – then the foot becomes the content, and the shoe the form.

Synthetic peoples are linear. They don't transflow, they only reflow. They are transportation people. For them, the foot is the content, and the shoe is the form, end of story. They can't comprehend the idea of the shoe as content and the foot as form, because their answer will always be: the foot goes inside the shoe. But it's not that simple. My foot determines the size of the shoe, not the other way around. Euro-Christian colonialists can only move forward and reflow, because they don't circulate like we do. Transportation comes and goes in a straight line.

In a cosmological system, there is no backflow. Water doesn't flow in reverse. It transflows. And by transflowing, it returns to where it came from in a cycle. It flows downstream, joins other waters, gains strength in the current, and at the same time, it evaporates; it travels elsewhere like a cloud, and it rains. The rain falls elsewhere but also returns to the springs. The springs emerge from the Cerrado and flow outward. Flowing and transflowing, they also evaporate and return as rain. They don't come back along the same path, the same route, or the same course. They move in a circular way. They transflow and conflow, but they don't reflow. Only in transportation is reflow possible: you come and go back.

Reflowing is only ever linear. When there is no circularity, you're forced to return the same way you came. In transflowing, there is no "going back" because it's circular. At the same time as something moves, it remains static; at the same time as it stays static, it moves –without getting disconnected.

We have a joke where the king asks a wise man, "Where is the end of the world?" The wise man puts his heel on the ground, curls his toes, turns his foot into a compass, draws a circle, and says, "The end of the world is right here, where my heel landed – because the world is round." Then the king asks, "And the beginning of the world?" "It's here too," the wise man replies. Here is the end and here is the beginning: it all depends on your position. We understand North and South differently from those who think in linear and vertical ways. For us, there's the side where the sun rises and the side where it sets. The side where the moon is born. The side the wind comes from, and the side it's moving toward.

Back when I was in school, they'd say: stand up, spread your arms. To your right is East, to your left is West, behind you is South … It was a way to orient ourselves. But if the place where I stand is the point of reference, then what's in front of me is North and behind me is

South. If I walk forward, that spot becomes South. If I walk backward, it becomes North. So North or South depends on where I am.

We've undergone a forceful and tightly structured process of colonization, one that has used politics in all its forms. But something interesting is happening now. Beings are beginning to speak of self-governance. We are living through a very special moment. We speak of cosmology instead of theory or ideology. We speak of territory instead of the factory. We speak of the village, the *quilombo*, the *terreiro*, instead of the workplace. The world of labor isn't the world being debated anymore. It isn't setting the agenda anymore. It's being replaced by the world of knowledge, by the world of lived experience.

Right now, we don't need to worry about politicians. We need to worry about the next generation. One day, I was riding my bike to the city with my nine-year-old granddaughter. She kept saying, "Grandpa, my bike is better than yours! I'm faster than you!" And she was right. Her bike is better, and she really is faster! But still, she gets scared when a car passes by. She has the energy, the speed, the skill, and I have my experience. We were conflowing, confluencing.

I prefer not to speak of dreams, but of imaginings, because dreams end when we wake up. In my imaginings, I'm in the background, confluencing in a supporting role for our granddaughter-generation. If I can keep dialoguing with that generation, I'm content. It's not worth expending energy on politicians; they've already been synthesized. Let's take care of the grand-daughter-generation, because they are the future. They are the present and the future, and we're here to be in conversation with them. The present is the interlocutor of the past and the speaker of the future. We must defend ourselves from the synthetic generation and help the new generation learn how to defend itself too.

Today's big debate is about decolonization, which I can only understand as the suppression of colonialism, its deterioration. I see the prefix "de-" as meaning depression, deterioration, decomposition. It is the job of decolonial people, wherever they are in the world, to educate their granddaughter-generation, not to attack mine. Decolonization is only necessary if it does that, because that's what's necessary now. For us, as counter-colonialists, our task is to inspire our granddaughter-generation to defend itself from the decolonial and the colonialists' granddaughter-generation. Because it's always important to defend oneself, but it's not necessary to attack right now. We don't need to destroy the colonialists. Let them live, so long as they live under their sun, and don't try to steal ours or take away our wind.

The world is vast, and there's space for everyone. The world is round precisely so people don't trample on one another.

Architecture and
Counter-Colonialism

"In Indigenous villages, and in *quilombos*, we carve out narrow paths," an Indigenous person once told me. "Sometimes they're less than a meter across. And the animals, jaguars, armadillos, and people take these paths. All living beings in the area take these paths without a problem, without attacking each other. The colonizers arrived, however, and widened these paths; they made them six meters wide, and soon only cars were using them. People didn't use them anymore, pigs and jaguars didn't either. Why did everything fit on our paths, which were only a meter wide, and on theirs, which are six meters wide, only one car fits?"

Indigenous people lived with a polytheistic cosmological system in Brazil. They lived cosmologically rather than with a humanist worldview. Then the Portuguese arrived with their version of humanity, and tried to apply it to our people's cosmologies. It didn't work. And so counter-colonialism arose. Counter-colonialism is simple: you want to colonize me, but I refuse to let you. I will defend myself. Counter-colonialism is a way of life that differs from colonialism.

African counter-colonial practice comes from Africa. It's a way of life that no one had named. We can speak of an Indigenous way of life, a *quilombo* way of life, a Bantu way of life, a Yoruba way of life. It'd be simple to say it like that. But if we do, we risk failing to weaken colonialism. We created the word "counter-colonialism" to weaken colonialism. Since one extreme defines the other, we turned colonialism against itself. We created an antidote: we're drawing the poison out of colonialism to transform it into an antidote to itself.

I was invited by sharers from the Complexo da Maré *favela* in Rio de Janeiro to discuss the relationship between the way people live in *quilombos* and the way people live in *favelas*. I was introduced to Maré and it was introduced to me. I had some very meaningful conversations with different groups there. We talked about what happened with the implementation of the *Minha Casa, Minha Vida* housing program.[1]

What's the most important part of a house in the *quilombo*? It's the *quintal*! In fact, there are many: the kitchen is important, for instance, because everyone comes in through the kitchen. But the *quintal* is essential because it's where the kids learn everything. And it's

---

[1] TR. A social housing program launched in 2009 under President Lula da Silva's first administration to finance and distribute affordable homes to low-income families in Brazil.

also where we save space to build a house for those who haven't been born yet, houses for future generations. In my daughter's house, for example, there's already space set aside to build a house for her child too. Our houses are designed with space for other houses.

If the *quintal* is essential to the *quilombo*, what's the most important part of a house in the *favela*? It's the *laje*.[2] The first *laje* is for the first-born son or daughter who gets married, and the second *laje* is for throwing parties. But what did *Minha Casa, Minha Vida* do? They came to the *favelas* and got rid of the *lajes*, the most important part of the houses. They came to the *quilombos* and built houses without *quintais*; they got rid of the *quintais*, the most important part of the houses.

Minha Casa, Minha Vida was the most colonial program in housing policy. It was a brutal, violent, cruel, racist, and institutionally colonial attack. It's better to say "colonialism" than "racism," because colonization changes the architecture; suppressing or banning the existing architecture is more than racism. Why don't they take the *favela* community's architecture into account?

Every house should be built with local natural materials; this is the first big issue. Every biome, every

---

[2] TR. In *favelas*, the *laje* – often a flat, open or semi-covered concrete surface – serves as more than just the top of the house. It becomes a shared space, used for gatherings, celebrations, and everyday family life.

environment, every place, offers us the conditions we need to live there. If I live in areas where there are coconut groves, then I use palm fronds to make the houses' roofs and to insulate their walls. If I don't want to use the leaves, I can use the central stems of the leaves. I can insulate the interior with woven mats; I can also make walls with rammed earth. I can build my house in the Caatinga just using material from the Caatinga; I can build my house in the Cerrado using only material from the Cerrado.

That's how we build houses in the *quilombos*. In the Cerrado, the houses are covered with *buriti* palm leaves, *babaçu* palm leaves, *piaçava* palm leaves, or other types of palm. In the Caatinga, the houses were once covered with *carnaúba* palm leaves, with the bark from certain trees, or even with tiles made of clay molded on our thighs and baked in the oven with dry wood from the area. The Caatinga has a lot of dry wood; we didn't even need to chop it. The houses were made from wattle and daub, or unfired clay bricks, stone, clay-rich earth, and wood. In coconut groves, houses were built of wattle and daub or rammed earth, with packed-earth floors, palm-thatched roofs, and doors made from the central stems of *babaçu* palm leaves. They were beautiful doors. When I was a kid, we used to make many doors from the central stems of *babaçu* palm leaves, but today my doors are made of iron. Now that I'm far from the coconut groves, I feel a deep nostalgia for those *babaçu* palm doors! It's the same in the Cerrado: people used doors, tables, chairs, and beds made from *buriti* palm. There was an incredible range of architectural styles.

For us, a house is the place where we're going to spend the better part of our lives. The house has to be part of our bodies. We have to sweat in that material, we have to feel our smells in our homes. Colonial architecture, a synthetic kind of architecture, doesn't let us do that. Those people need to make houses with smooth, flat, linear walls.

Colonial architecture eliminates art, since it's a mechanized mode of knowing; it isn't handmade, it has no life.

In the cities, since the plots of land are small, narrow, and long, the houses are also built in a longitudinal form. They're built with the highest ridges of the roof facing the road and the shortest parts facing the neighboring plots. The doors are positioned on the higher sides of the roof and the windows under the slopes. That way, when it rains, the water falls on either side of the window. In most *quilombo* houses, the rainwater flows toward the door. In the *Minha Casa, Minha Vida* housing program, however, the rainwater was designed to drain toward the windows. These houses have neither space nor a sense of territoriality. They're elongated houses. The more you build, the less space you have.

It's different from houses designed in a transversal way, where the water falls over the door, letting me make the house larger to the left and right, to the front or back, without needing a hallway.

In our houses, the door is under the roof's slope, not on the high side. The window is often next to the door. The living room is built with openings on both sides, so we don't need a hallway. You can make the house bigger on whatever side you want, and it's generally a big, spacious, and welcoming house. There's a bedroom on each side, a living room in the middle, and a kitchen extending out from it – that's another valuable thing.

In *quilombo* architecture, the kitchen is the biggest space. It's a space where we welcome guests. Anyone who comes inside goes to the kitchen. In the *quilombos*, although it doesn't seem like it, the more women are in the kitchen, the more power they have. When they're cooking, they aren't alone: whoever comes into the kitchen helps with the cooking. The women organize the space. They grab a squash and someone will say, "Let me cut up the squash!" They grab parsley and scallions and someone will say, "Let me make a salad!" They don't tell anyone to do anything; they start making food and people join in and keep the conversation going. The men come in and show off their workshops, their work, their *roça*... The highlight of the celebration is the food: it's what brings everyone together. And whoever cooked conducts that grand moment. It's the opposite of what you'd think. It's not a stressful activity. Cooking is only exhausting when you cook alone to serve everyone. In a festive atmosphere, cooking isn't stressful at all.

The kitchen is the best place in *quilombo* architecture; it's the most important and the best kept. If someone comes to my house and goes into the living room, no one will greet them in the living room. There's no such thing for us. Everyone goes to the kitchen! The architecture is also designed around food. Food makes the party, it sets the tone for how we welcome others. Everything is organized around food. In our architecture, we think about food and celebrations, about shared forms of life.

In the *favelas*, *laje* construction happens in a similar way. Some people will make the food, others will make the concrete. Everyone will do something.

This is what a *laje* is: you go into the *favela* at the end of the week and everyone wants to have a barbeque on the *laje*. For us, food is essential; we never handle it in a petty way. Sometimes, when we go inside some monotheistic, Euro-Christian people's apartments, we realize that food is treated like it's forbidden. They even hide food from guests! It's like saying, "Oh, they only came to eat, it's like they're dying of hunger, like they don't eat at home or don't know how high the cost of living is!" Now for us, it's exactly the opposite: "They came in and didn't eat? I made a chicken and they wouldn't eat it?" It's disrespectful if a person comes to our home and doesn't eat our food.

When I was growing up, the fences were all made of wood. When we cleared land for a *roça*, we'd begin by cutting the thinnest, most scattered undergrowth, which didn't even work as firewood, and we'd put it out to dry. That wood worked for making fences. We'd cut off the ends of the wood to separate them from the leaves so they wouldn't stop the fire from reaching the dry branches we wanted to burn. When we found firewood, the kind that would last a long time on the ground (*aroeira, jatobá, angico*, Caatinga woods), we'd separate it so it didn't burn out too quickly, just singe. We'd also separate the wood that was for sawing into planks, and we'd remember if someone would be married the next year. We'd think, "Let's ask if they'll need wood to make a door, a bench, to make furniture." If someone needed it, they could just grab it. We were always very careful about sorting out different types of wood.

When we were kids and we'd go for a walk in the woods, we'd mark the places where we'd build our houses, and one of the first conditions was for there to be shade. We'd mark the spot close to a very shady tree, because there would be guaranteed shelter there, or we'd watch the sun rise and set to understand its pathway, so as to put the house in a position that would have shade in the morning or afternoon. Since we live in the Caatinga, we need to observe the stars and find guaranteed shade. The question of wind is also fundamental: we have to think about what side to put the door on, if there's going to be a lot of dust or not, if there'll be ventilation so it doesn't get so hot. This is all a matter of how we relate to nature.

We'd go to see the stars in the *terreiro*, because at the beginning of the night it's important to see the moon – whether it's waxing, waning, or new – and see the stars. A house is built according to the terrain, the placement of its door and windows, and the position of the moon. A house is all of these things. You plot your house into the land, but you also plot your house into the stars, so that it fits into a cosmological relationship – how far it is from your *roça*, from the roads, from the neighbors.

There are two types of neighbors. First, neighbors who are siblings, who live nearby, who can hear movement in each other's houses. If something strange happens in my sibling's house, I'll hear it from here. Next, there are the neighbors who aren't siblings and are at least a shout away. In the time when there weren't telephones, this was a good distance for people to be able to hear a cry for help, an invitation to a party … or for when a child was born, or the sound of fireworks reaching as many neighbors as possible.

In debates about "asphalt" and *favelas*, people usually say that we live in isolation in the *favelas* and in the *quilombos*. We then say that people are isolated in Alphaville,[3] but there's a very valuable difference, and we pose a provocative challenge: what if people from Alphaville just lived off of what's in Alphaville without asking for anything from elsewhere, and what if in the *quilombos* we just lived off what's in the *quilombos*? People from Alphaville say that we're poor and they have resources, but who will have the means to live longer: us or the Alphaville residents?

They also say that there's militia and organized crime in the *favelas* and in the *quilombos*. What we say is that there's militia in Alphaville. The difference is that the Alphaville militia is legalized and institutionalized, and far more heavily armed than the *favela* militias. What they call "private security" is a militia. The militias in the *favelas* are mostly made up of retired, discharged, or even active military personnel. And who owns the private security companies? The military. The military is the largest industry of violence in colonialist society. Because they are funded by society to stop the violence, they get paid by the

---

[3] TR. The Alphaville gated communities are a series of upscale private housing developments that emerged in the state of São Paulo in the 1970s.

Alphaville middle class to stop the violence, and they get paid by people from the *favelas* to stop the violence!

Who is more ethical? Gangs of robbers or military gangs? The military gangs make money off of stopping the robberies, and the gangs of robbers are paid through their robberies. There's a group who is paid to rob and a group who is paid to stop the robbery. What's the difference? The group who is paid to rob only receives a payment when the action is performed. A robber who doesn't rob doesn't get paid, but the police who get paid to prevent the robbery get their money whether or not they stop anything. Now, each time there's a robbery, the police should return the thing that was stolen to the victim, because they're paid to prevent robberies. If they don't prevent the robbery and they get paid anyway, then they're getting paid for a service they didn't provide. What's the name for this? And why does the middle class celebrate, cheering for the police? How could you brag about supporting a police force that profits from preventing robbery and profits from facilitating robbery? This is a debate we urgently need to have. And we need to discuss public security policies.

If someone asks me if our books are reaching the *quilombos*, I reply that they're not made for *quilombos*. Our books leave the *quilombos* and have to reach

Alphaville, to reach the universities and malls. In the *quilombos*, we live through oral tradition; we build our knowledge on the street corners, in the neighborhood bars. We make these kinds of comparisons in the bar on the side of the road, and we laugh when an all-powerful car passes by and closes its window in fear. We laugh, as if to say, "Poor guy, he's a prisoner in his Alphaville, and still a prisoner on the street when he sees us!" We're people who arrest without handcuffs or keys, just from our appearance. We make this comparison in bars, at wakes, while fishing, when it's just us. If they're talking about us, we're going to talk a bit about them too.

After the wind farms and solar power plants and high-voltage power lines arrived (the so-called "development"), violence arrived too. I live five kilometers from a city where everything changed when these ways of life arrived. Even so, I can still leave my motorcycle on the sidewalk when I get home late and only put it away the next day. I can still sleep in the city plazas/squares, a city with a population of twenty thousand, where it's common for a person to come up and ask how I'm doing or if I want them to bring me home. This kind of relationship doesn't exist in Alphaville. We still share with each other.

There's also forced sharing in big cities. Sometimes, there's someone who has the means to have more than a phone and they walk around carelessly with the phone in their hand, and then along comes a boy and grabs the phone. This is forced sharing, but it doesn't stop being a mode of sharing. The boy knows that that person can buy another phone – or if they can't, that they've already used it for a while, and now it's his turn to use it too.

It doesn't matter if there are thieves in the *favela*, if there are militias in the *favela*; what matters to us is knowing if there are people in the *favela*, and if these people communicate with us. I'm not the police. I don't need to know if a person is a thief or not, if a person is honest or dishonest. What's much more interesting is thinking about how we're going to care for another life when it's in need of care.

Just look at the perversity of colonialism: in Piauí, the *Fome Zero* program[4] was launched in two towns: Guaribas and Acauã. Government officials got to Guaribas by helicopter because there wasn't a place to land a plane or an easy way to get there by car. The people wanted the sand road to the city of Caracóis, which is less than a hundred kilometers away, to be paved.

The brown howler monkey, known in Brazil as *guariba*, gets discriminated against: it's a monkey that yells too much, that shits too much, nobody likes the

[4] TR. Referred to as a zero-hunger strategy, this 2003 program launched by President Lula da Silva aimed to address chronic food insecurity and extreme poverty.

brown howler monkey. It's one of the monkeys most hunted for its meat. Nobody likes it, but the brown howler monkey is one of the smartest monkeys: when a human being points a gun at a *guariba* mother, she grabs her baby and puts it in her lap, showing the human that she's nursing. She does! And when a human being shoots, the monkey takes a leaf and presses it to the wound to try to stop the bleeding. It knows how to stop the bleeding with a leaf, but even so, the human being shoots again and kills it.

Guaribas was considered the poorest city in Brazil because it didn't have either restaurants or hotels. But Guaribas had neither restaurants nor hotels because restaurants and hotels are places for poor people. We rich people don't need restaurants and hotels, because we welcome people into our homes. The people of Guaribas welcome others into their homes, not into restaurants.

When I arrived in Rio de Janeiro, I didn't know any restaurants, hotels, or snack bars. That wasn't part of my life. I knew what a kitchen was. And a place to sleep was simply the house I was visiting. In most towns in the state of Piauí, it was rare to see a hotel or restaurant before 1992. Where, then, was food sold in these towns? In the street markets. On the street market days, people would come to make food for people who were traveling. It wasn't for the people from the city, it was for the traveling salesmen, the bank owners ...

People always had relatives in the city and went to eat at their relatives' houses. We'd tease them when someone at the street market offered food to someone from the same city. "When you went to my house, I didn't sell you food, so why are you selling it to me?"

When people from the city visited the communities, they didn't buy food, and when we went to the city, we ate in their houses. Since we knew city folks had almost never had *roças*, we brought (and we still bring) food to prepare. We hold an Umbanda gathering in the Custaneira Quilombo, in the town of Paquetá in Piauí. One of the elders sets the date and people arrive two days beforehand with rice, beans, corn, tapioca, flour, dried meat, *rapadura*, and eggs. Each person brings what they have or what they can and offers it to the kitchen, which is big and full of people to receive it. And there are also people who just help make the food so that everyone eats, everyone drinks, and there's no need for a restaurant. Restaurant food is never that good. Sometimes it's cold or reheated, sometimes it's even gone bad. We don't trust food for sale; all food for sale is dangerous. Why does humanity need restaurants? Because they're afraid to welcome people into their homes. They're afraid of people! Humans are afraid of themselves. This is cosmophobia.

When the federal government reached Guaribas, they could have asked the people what they wanted, if the people wanted anything. Why didn't they ask? In São Raimundo Nonato, which is one hundred kilometers from Canto do Buriti, castor beans were cultivated. It's one of the places with the longest tradition of growing this crop. If they wanted to plant castor beans to make biodiesel, they could have asked the locals how to do it! But no, they chose to plant it in places where it had never been grown before. Various administrations came and went before Guaribas had a paved road. It was what the residents most wanted, but it took a long time for the governments to build it. Even though volleyball and basketball weren't played there, they built a volleyball court and a basketball court first. They even built a hotel. The hotel and the courts were all abandoned. People rejected them all.

Who normally makes up the Ministry of Agrarian Development? Primarily people from the South of Brazil. People from the Caatinga aren't represented proportionally. What works as technical guidance for people from the South of Brazil doesn't work for us. How can they advise those who practice free-raising when they themselves raise animals in captivity? How can they advise those who plant crops inside fences when their own practice is to plant in open fields?

I live next to Serra da Capivara National Park, and just on the other side is the Lagoas Quilombo, which is home to more than 1,500 families, close to ten thousand people. It's approximately 70,000 hectares, which is nothing if we divide it by 1,500 families. But the government claimed that the *quilombolas* had too much land and gave a mining company a license within this territory without complying with the national and international consultation protocols. In practice, there isn't a big difference between left-wing and right-wing administrations. The State itself is a colonial framework. A colonial and abstract framework.

There's no such thing as a good government within a bad State. Just like there's no good driver for a broken-down car, or a good conductor for a failing train. Whatever administration governs this state will be a colonial government, because the State is colonialist. A person who rides a bike is a cyclist, and a person who drives a car is a driver. To be a colonialist is like being an ox handler. Whatever government rules a colonial state will be a colonial government. We must counter-colonize the entire organizing structure.

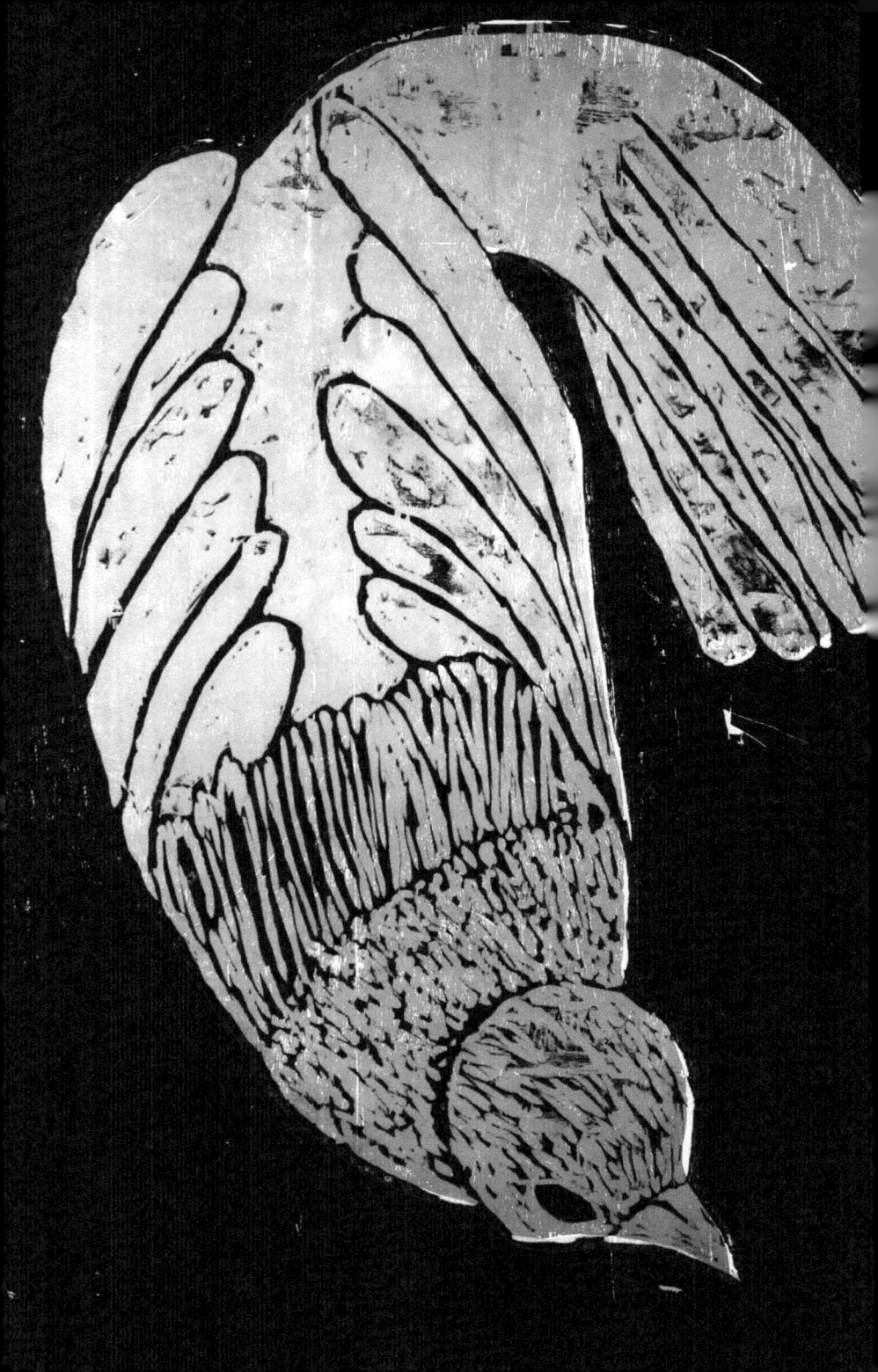

Colonialism of Submission

The Caatinga is an incredibly rich and vibrant environment. Every plant in the Caatinga is edible, medicinal, or forageable. Every single plant is necessary. There isn't one that isn't. The dried leaves of *gafavera*,[1] *aroeira*,[2] and *juá*, for example, contain more protein than soy or corn. Why do we see Caatinga plants without any leaves, yet the animals are still fat? Why do wild animals live – and thrive – in the Caatinga? Because the plants are extremely rich in nutrients. Yet the Euro-Christian rulers, our politicians who live in the Caatinga, hide this. They only speak about the negative aspects of the Caatinga. They say there's hunger here, that the rainy season isn't enough to grow beans, rice, or corn.

Where I live, *umbu* is grown on a large scale. Anything you can make with grapes you can make with *umbu*;

[1] TR. Likely a reference to the *favela* or *faveleira* tree (*Cnidoscolus quercifolius*), known for its protein-rich seeds and medicinal leaves.
[2] TR. *Aroeira* is a vernacular name used for different tree species in Brazil. Depending on context, it may refer to the pink pepper tree (*Schinus terebinthifolius*), whose berries are used as a spice and in traditional remedies, or to *Myracroduron urundeuva* (often known as *aroeira-do-sertão*), a hardwood species.

or, rather, anything you make with grapes can also be made with *umbu*. In Piauí, we've had a Grape Festival, but we've never had an Umbu Festival. *Cajuína*, a wonderful natural-sugar soft drink and a historical and cultural heritage of people from Piauí, doesn't have a festival dedicated to it on the same scale as the Grape Festival. Politicians want to appease the people of the Brazilian South and Southeast so they can feel closer to them.

We often talk about universal colonialism, but there's also a colonialism of submission. This is a colonialism enacted not by the powerful, but by those already subjugated, who reproduce domination downward. They treat the Caatinga as if it were something harmful, something to be fought. You see northeastern governors going down South, begging with a tin cup, asking for money to "combat" the Caatinga. That's what I call colonialism of submission. It's the colonialist who is submissive to other colonialists, in the same way that other Brazilian colonialists are submissive to the colonialists from the countries of the North.

My mother passed into the realm of the ancestors at eighty-four years old and never had to leave the Caatinga. There are still people alive today, at over a hundred years old, who have never needed to leave the Caatinga. So how can anyone say the Caatinga isn't a good place to live? The politicians who live here may reside in the Caatinga, but they are not of the Caatinga. They're not sharers, not *caatingueiros*. Why are we eating wheat bread when the Caatinga gives us corn? We should be eating corn bread. When there's cassava, we should be eating *beiju* or cassava porridge. There's no need to replace local food with products from the Brazilian Southeast just because of colonialism of submission.

When I was born, probably two-thirds of the so-called "human population" lived in what's called "the rural world" – what colonial language refers to as "the countryside." Back then, what we produced, gathered, and cultivated from the land was enough to feed ourselves. And the surplus was enough to feed those in the cities, because the cities were small. Since more than two-thirds of the population could feed itself, it was simple to supply the remaining third. Transporting food to the cities could be done with animal-drawn carts. We only needed to carry essentials to that one-third of the population and we needed to bring very little back, because we produced nearly everything we needed. Transport by animals was effective. We didn't need cars, only ox carts for carrying things that were too heavy for animals or people to manage. Our transportation always used organic energy.[3]

I used to walk about nine kilometers to school. I studied at night and worked in the *roça* during the day.

---

[3] TR. "*Energia orgânica*" is likewise unusual in the Portuguese.

I'd run because there wasn't much time, but sometimes, if I passed a *pequi* tree,[4] I'd pick the fruit and take it to relatives in the city. I picked fruit on the way home, fed myself, played, watched the birds, bathed in the stream. My life was paradise. That wasn't work. That was living. We were simply living. There was no need for planning, only confluences.

When agribusiness arrived, they told us to stop eating many of the fruits we used to consume. Everything that wasn't a commodity was deemed worthless. Only what could be sold had value.

Back then, fruit wasn't something you bought at a market. My grandmother used to say, "Whoever sells watermelon, sells piss." Our people were ashamed to sell watermelon, mango, cashew, *pequi*, or *umbu*. If nature gives it to you for free, why sell it? That's pure colonialism. Colonialism starts by saying that our type of mango isn't good and then sells a different kind – Tommy mangoes, those shipped-in "airplane" mangoes. So every good mango has to reach us by plane now?

To harvest *pequi*, we used to wait for it to fall from the tree, because if you pick it, the flesh doesn't separate as easily from the spiny pit. With cashews, we'd pick the nicest ones and leave the rest for the birds; whatever

---

[4] TR. *Pequi* (*Caryocar brasiliense*) is a large tree native to Brazil, known for its oily, aromatic fruits.

fell on the ground was for the pigs. We never took all of it. But then the colonialists replaced the seeds, and the animals, too.

People talk about racism, but they usually limit that conversation to the human species. The issue, however, is much broader. Just think about the variety of fish we used to have, and how few remain today. Now, when people talk about fish, they mean tambaqui[5] or tilapia. In some places, fish that aren't farm-raised aren't even considered fish anymore. If you offer someone a wild-caught fresh-water fish, they don't want it. They only want tambaqui or tilapia: that is, fish that have been synthesized.[6] If you offer someone *banana-roxa*[7] or *banana-da-terra*,[8] they don't want it; they only want *pacovan* or *prata*.[9] Fruit is being reduced to just one or two kinds. Racism exists

---

[5] TR. A large tropical freshwater species (*Colossoma macropomum*) originally from the Amazon basin, now commonly produced through aquaculture in regions far from its native environment.

[6] TR. Farm-raised fish, in other words.

[7] TR. A lesser-known Brazilian banana variety distinguished by its purplish skin and slightly tangy flavor, often eaten raw or used in local preparations. Known in English as red banana or red dacca.

[8] TR. Plantain, a starchy, large banana variety commonly used for cooking in Brazil, especially fried or baked.

[9] TR. Two of the most widely consumed large banana cultivars in Brazil. Pacovan is known for its firm texture and culinary use, while prata is known for its sweetness and smooth consistency when eaten raw.

against all forms of life: against types of fruit, fish species, and even wild animals, whose numbers are shrinking.

An Afro-confluent hunter from the town of Dom Inocêncio once told me: "If IBAMA[10] actually paid attention, they wouldn't ban hunting! If they understood that goats and deer eat the same things, they'd let us eat venison. We'd have smaller goat herds because we'd have deer in the forest available for food." But since we're not allowed to hunt deer, we've increased the number of goats, which then compete with the deer for food. As a result, the deer starve. Because in addition to the goats in the forest, our presence itself disrupts the way deer feed. We make noise, we put bells on the goats, we change the environment. IBAMA should ask us what we do about food. Because we don't just eat deer meat. One day it might be deer, another day it might be another kind of game. And sometimes there's no meat at all because we don't eat meat every day. I grew up eating meat only on weekends. The rest of the time, we had fish, eggs, and fruit.

I've never seen a campaign to collect water for wild animals in the Caatinga. NGOs don't run donation drives to provide food for wildlife during the droughts

[10] TR. Brazil's federal environmental agency, which is responsible for enforcing environmental policy and overseeing the protection of the country's natural heritage.

in the Northeast. They only think about humans, cattle, and pets. If we were allowed to raise domestic animals in our traditional way, our animals wouldn't compete with wild ones, and the wild species would thrive. The wildlife is starving because it can't withstand the competition. And along with the domestic animals come the human beings. My hunter friend's insight is brilliant!

Neither IBAMA nor environmental activists talk about this. How many domestic animals can the Caatinga provide for without displacing wildlife? Hunters never hunted pregnant animals, at least not back when hunting was still allowed. When we trap an animal, we can tell if it's male or female, pregnant or not – and if necessary, we let it go. A hunter wouldn't kill a young female knowing that the future depends on her.

When we catch fish in traps, we can sort them, separating the larger ones from the smaller ones. A good fisherman can even tell the males from the females, and if it's spawning season, he'll release the female. There's an entire body of knowledge involved. So many things have never been thoughtfully discussed with hunters, because if there were conversations, people would realize it's not as bad as it's made out to be. There is, in fact, a kind of informal contract.

While I was plowing the land, my great-uncle once told me, "The ox doesn't need to work to eat. You need the ox. So, ask nicely instead of yelling at him!" The ox can choose whether to help or not, but if you insist and reason with him without getting violent, he'll respond. We treat animals with care because we know we depend on them.

When you're hunting clandestinely, whatever you catch, you take, because you're afraid you won't catch anything else. But when hunting was permitted and you caught a pregnant animal, you'd release it because you believed you'd catch another one later. Today, it feels more like stealing. You take the first animal you get because you're afraid IBAMA will catch you.

If you don't want people to hunt, then create other jobs. Pay hunters a minimum wage during breeding season – just like you pay fishermen during spawning season. Where are the so-called "progressive" politicians who should have something to say about this? It's time for them to speak up. And why do the environmental activists and NGOs merely denounce hunters? These same activists and NGO workers come into our homes, eat our food, even hunt alongside us, but once they leave, they criticize the hunters.

IBAMA only goes after hunters – not the people involved in clear-cutting. In Chapada Grande, tens of thousands of hectares were deforested. How many armadillos and deer lived there? Organic relationships are being disrespected.

In the 1970s, every puddle of water had fish in it. We used to say fish were falling from the River Jordan, that fish were falling from the sky! There were fish everywhere, birds and game everywhere. My grandmother used to say that just like the best place to keep fish is in the river, the best place to keep cassava roots is underground.

But then they started spraying poison, and the wild animals began to die. You spray poison on an insect, it dies – but so do the animals that eat it.

There aren't any more fish in the rivers because they spray poison on the crops during *piracema* – the fish spawning season. When the first rains come, the water flows back to the springs and kills both large and small fish, disrupting reproduction. It's a large-scale massacre. They built huge dams and caused the rivers to silt up. They cleared the forests, and now organic matter no longer flows into the rivers. The waters that once carried organic matter now carry poison instead. Where are the biology and veterinary science professors – the scholars – to take this on? Where are the dissertations that address this? It would be easy to prove. This is a necessary debate, but it's a debate universities are too afraid to face.

We need to dismantle the myth that we're the ones destroying the environment, that we're responsible for extinction, that hunters are to blame. Why don't they blame Aldrin 40, DDT, or other poisons? Because the laboratories funded the universities to conduct the research, and many people whose work depended on that funding blamed us instead.

But now it's becoming clear: it's not our responsibility. The chemical monoculture, which robs other living beings of their food, is responsible.

Free Raising, Fenced Planting

In our community, most Afro-confluent families rely on agriculture. No one owned land; we cultivated it. If we planted a *roça* one year, we would use that area in a cycle for two years. In the first year, we'd plant everything together. Corn, cassava, beans, and cotton were planted together in the same *roça*. We didn't plant crops in lines; we planted them in a triangular form, because a linear form wouldn't be possible where there were tree stumps. With a triangular approach, we could plant between the stumps, and the native plants would grow among the crops.

Many living beings would come to eat the native plant leaves and end up helping us protect the crops. When there's only one type of crop and we don't let the native plants grow, these beings eat everything that is planted. That's why we started needing to use poison. Agricultural Sciences only reached our community in the 1970s. Before then, we didn't have any livestock technicians or agronomists. We planted various types of seeds together because we were governed by the guidance of the cosmos.

Our grandmother-generation would say that we plant what we want, what we need, and what we love, and the Earth gives what it can and what we deserve.

So, we would sow all kinds of seeds on the same plot and the land selected the seeds that it would let sprout. Some animals known as insects preferred eating a certain type of plant and left others alone. This was our people's cosmological wisdom. We didn't need to use poison because animals made the selections. Since all the plants were edible, whatever remained was ours to harvest.

Our people would also say that the Earth gives and the Earth wants.[1] When we say this, we're not talking about the Earth in and of itself, but about the Earth and all of its sharers. As for triangular planting, when the waters come, the currents run into one plant and flow toward another. The plants slow down the flow of the water. When the Agricultural Sciences arrived, however, they started teaching us to plant and plow in rows. But when wind or water comes, they rush through the furrows and just wash everything away, because there isn't anything to break the current. To make matters worse, we were instructed to plant just one crop in each plot. We knew, nevertheless, that if we planted just one kind of seed in a given area, the beings that were used to eating a variety of plants would eat just that one thing.

Another difference has to do with cycles. We planted crops with various cycles. We grilled and ate the

[1] TR. Earth/earth: see p. 29, n. 1.

short-cycle corn, which matured quickly; they let the longer-cycle corn grow taller to produce more grassland for animals to graze.

We planted sweet cassava, known as *macaxeira*, which had a six-month cycle, but we also planted another cassava with a two-year cycle. We harvested one and the other would remain in the ground. Everything was planned, but the Agricultural Sciences arrived and taught us to plant just short-cycle species, and to harvest them as quickly as possible.

Nobody did soil analysis. We just knew the soil by sight. We would know what to plant just by looking at the land. We knew the vegetation. On land where a lot of native legumes grow, we'd plant beans; on land where a lot of native grasses grow, we'd plant corn and rice. It's a cosmic language. It's simple. No need for soil analysis because the Earth already tells us what it's ready to offer.

When we'd clear the land for planting, first we'd pull the weeds, remove the dry branches, and let the vegetation dry for a spell. When we were planning a burn, we'd cut down the thick vegetation fifteen days before setting the fire. Fifteen days later, we'd do the burn based on where the sun was, because the underbrush served as a bed for the fire. The thick vegetation would fall on top, and the fire would just burn the leaves, the brush, and the useless wood.

The thick wood, which was still green, would just sweat. We cleared out the hard woods, like the *aroeira*, before the fire. We also cleared out the forked trunks that could support beams for the houses. These trunks were perennial, and we used the wood to build tables or doors too. We'd lightly singe the white wood (the kind without heartwood) to make it last longer. The pieces that were singed but not burned through were used to fence our *roças*.

There's only one rainy season for the crops with six-month cycles. After that, we harvest these crops. The dry straw stays in the soil to fertilize the land for the crops with two-year cycles, like cassava, cotton, and castor beans. In the second year, we harvest the longer-cycle crops. The white wood likewise only lasts for two years. After that, it doesn't work for the fences. That's why we would take down the fences and then use the wood as firewood for the cassava flour ovens and the boilers used to make *rapadura* sugar.

I'm not talking about sugarcane monoculture. In our *quilombos* in Piauí, this didn't exist like it did in other northeastern states in Brazil. Here, there was large-scale cattle ranching. But few of our people raised cattle. We raised pigs, goats, and sheep, and we used oxen for transportation.

In those times, there were no banks to deposit money in, but the Euro-Christian colonialists used oxen as banks. They kept cattle as an economic reserve. A calf could live up to ten years, and oxen were considered fully grown. People only killed them when they needed money. They "aged" the cattle on the *chapada*,[2] and when it was necessary, they only sold them as a herd. My great-grandfather and my great-uncle were master negotiators with the ranchers. They'd say, "You give us ten males and I'll raise them for you. I'll get the calf and give it to you once it's ten. For those ten years, they'll work for me." What we did was get the rancher's cattle and benefit from their labor while they grew. The calves that were coming of age ate cane straw, which wasn't a monoculture. We used to plant sugarcane in the areas we called *vazantes* – the floodplains, the wet soils. In the middle of the sugarcane fields, we also planted bananas, tubers, pumpkins, and sweet cassava. While we were involved in the work of caring for the sugarcane, we also had other food we could eat.

Even today, in Piauí's Caatinga, crops are planted inside fences, while animals are raised in freedom. There isn't an official system that regulates this practice. The Civil Code says that the animal's owner has to tie

---

[2] TR. In Brazil, "*chapada*" refers to an extensive flat-topped plateau, landscapes often associated with cattle grazing and small-scale farming.

it up, and that's why most states' crops are planted in unfenced fields and animals are raised in captivity. Their logic is that animals roam, and you must tie up whatever roams. We do the opposite here. We fence in the plants, which don't move, and we let the animals roam free.

We have an understanding – and this is cosmological – that everything born of nature belongs to everyone. The native pastures are shared, and the Caatinga is made up of native pastures. So people from here can raise animals even if they aren't documented landowners. They raise them on the land the ranchers say is theirs. And everyone agrees with this; there isn't any conflict. What you can't do is plant! To plant, the ranchers will charge rent for the land.

In Dom Inocêncio, one of the towns with the largest amount of goat and sheep farming in Piauí, there are no pastures or grasses. Fences almost don't exist there, and different animals are raised together. In our *quilombo*, our goats are also raised all together. They know where to go at the end of the day, but if one ends up on someone else's property, we return it. Here, no one steals anybody else's goats. We take joy in giving them back, and if we find another owner's animal and it's sick, we take care of it.

With the arrival of agribusiness and colonialist customs, it's become impossible to raise animals freely in certain regions, which has made everything much harder. Chapada Grande, for example, is part of the Cerrado bordering the Berlengas River and is enormously diverse. During the winter, we bring the animals there because it's elevated. And in the summer, our animals come down into the Berlengas Valley. It was always like this. In Chapada Grande, there were so much *fava-de-bolota*[3] – a highly nutritious pom-pom-shaped leguminous species – that the animals didn't eat it all. We would even gather a bit to sell. And this happened up until recently, in the twenty-first century. But then soybean and eucalyptus farmers arrived. They cleared thousands of hectares. They planted crops and banned people from the town from raising animals freely, but no one was prepared to keep them in captivity. Cattle ranching ended in Chapada Grande, and so did extractivism.

A way of life ended – the way of life in the place I was born. Chapada Grande had an infinity of plants, the forest was full of fruit and animals; it was a life woven through sharing. These lives were attacked and destroyed, and the ways of life that made sharing possible also ceased to exist. What happened to the

---

[3] TR. "*Fava-de-bolota*" is a drought-resistant leguminous plant native to the Brazilian Caatinga, used for animal feed and other traditional purposes.

people who knew how to live like that? When we take the jaguar's food away and stand in front of it, what's it going to do?

Development and colonialism started subjugating, attacking, destroying. When development is imposed on spaces where the people live through involvement, when ways of life are attacked, when community is atrophied, rendered invisible, and fractured, there's going to be a reaction. What are the consequences of destroying an environment's conditions of existence? The beings that belong to this environment are going to want to live in a different environment. Since they aren't prepared to live in other environments, they'll have to prepare. The new environment will determine how they'll prepare. In Chapada Grande, the world people knew ended and it was transformed into a world of eucalyptus and soybeans. Development took away the local youth's imagination. People were raised to live in one world only to end up in another. Chapada Grande was a place where there were no muggings and robberies, but today it's become dangerous. When an ATM is installed, it's bound to get blown up at some point. They took away the jaguar's food, and now we're facing the consequences.

The Caatinga is the most resistant biome we have because it's full of rocks. It has an irregular physical geography and short vegetation. This is why it was never interesting for agribusiness. The *chapada* territories, which are also part of this confluence, are indeed interesting for agribusiness. But today, the territories that we thought would be preserved are in fact being attacked by wind farms and photovoltaic power. How can they say that wind farms are low impact, that they're about renewable, sustainable, ecological energy? In the town of Queimada Nova in Piauí, five *quilombola* communities of ours have been attacked by wind power plants. The Queimada Nova mountains now have huge wind turbines on them. Not even the snakes stayed there. The snakes came down from the mountains, peccaries came down, the wild pigs came down and are attacking the communities and the *roças*. There are corn fields that were totally devastated by the wild pigs and peccaries that had lost their environments.

The animal exodus has to do with fencing and the environmental transformation caused by the capturing of the wind and sun's rays, but mainly it has to do with deforestation. Deforestation opens up enormous clearings, and the wildlife isn't accustomed to them. The exodus has to do with the loud noises wind turbines make. It has to do with the new human presence there. We have to fence in and tie up our animals because they can't keep wandering around these areas and because there's been a significant reduction in natural pastures. For us, what was once native forage and food for the animals was turned into food for the machines. Local vegetation now feeds the machines and generates electricity for the cities. What was food for living beings, for our sustenance, is now food for the big cities.

This is the essence of colonialism. And there are still people who say colonialism is over! They took the brazilwood[4] and now, when there isn't any more wood to take, they take the wind and the sun. They are extracting synthesized wind and synthesized sun in the form of electricity. Here in Piauí, in Rio Grande do Norte, and in other northeastern states, we have dunes on the coast. But in Tocantins there are dunes in the Cerrado, in the middle of the arid plateau zones. The direction the wind blows will change because of the enormous wind turbines built on top of the hills. How will this affect the dunes? The wind turbines change the direction of the wind. In some places, the wind will become weaker, and in others, stronger. Some living beings depend on the wind. Without it, how will they move? How will synthesized wind impact the bees' movements? People really aren't paying attention to this. They're stealing our wind; they're stealing our sun. This is no joke.

[4] TR. "*Pau-brasil*" is a name historically used for certain tropical hardwoods prized for their reddish dye.

Ecology is a word used by academics. In the *quilombo*, there's no such thing as "ecology." There are the *roças* of the *quilombo*, of Indigenous villages, of riverside communities, of shellfish gatherers and fishermen, and of nut-breakers. Why does academia use the word *ecology* and not *quilombola agriculture*? Why not say *Indigenous roça*? Universities are factories that transform knowledge into commodities, and *quilombola* agriculture isn't a commodity. But the knowledge considered valid is the knowledge the university commodifies.

When I visited the Kalunga Quilombo in Goiás, I went on a hike for tourists. There, I saw a sign next to a trash can that said, "Organic Waste." I asked why that bin was for "Organic Waste." They replied that it was an environmental policy. Well now, if it's organic, it's not trash! Trash is synthetic! Things that rot are organic and return to the earth to nourish it, like my grandmother taught us. But this only makes sense to people who have homes, not to people who live in cages called apartments. Discussing ecology without discussing architecture is delusional.

We invented the *quilombo roça*, but universities changed this name and now they want to sell us our knowledge, offering us courses on agroecology and on building houses with rammed earth. We eat *macambira* roots and *umbu* roots, among many others, and they say we're savages because we eat roots. Today, they've

changed the names of our roots: they call them "uncon-
ventional edible plants." What they call a cherry tomato
was a very tasty little sour tomato that sprang up
wherever we went. We used to make rice with the *cuxá*
plant, which they now call hibiscus. They invented
"organic food." Now, what you buy in the supermarket with the "organic" seal is a product, which is
sometimes grown without poison, but it's not organic.
It's not produced by organic knowledge; it's not oriented
towards life. If a kilo of organic meat is very expensive,
poor folks can't buy it; and if the poor can't eat it, it's
not organic. What's organic, what is truly of the earth, is
what all life forms can access. If life can't access it, then
it's not organic. It's a commodity, whether it's poison
or not.

Colonialist tactics like these try to deceive us by
turning our knowledge into commodities. Meanwhile,
humans are the only animals that need to study after
they reach adulthood. After they leave the nest, birds
already know what they need to know in order to live.
Once they're grown, rodents already know everything
they need to know to live. That's how it is with all other
living beings except humans: food cures them and
prevents diseases …

Other animals only get sick when they're in contact
with humans. Why did we get less sick in the *quilombos*
during the pandemic? A great elder explains: "In

quilombos, we have relationships. We don't have crowds. Crowds are made up of bodies that don't know each other, that don't touch each other." And because they don't interact, they're not immune. For us, we who interact, we who embrace each other, we're immune.

We are people of lived experience, not abstract theories. We are circular: beginning, middle, and beginning. Our lives don't end. A grandmother-generation is the beginning, a mother-generation is the middle, and a granddaughter-generation is the beginning again.

Untitled

A bishop, a knight, and a rook
Who moves against infinity
And risks themselves in the fight
Gathers king, pawn, and queen
Who takes the knife from its sheath
And scratches earth and ground
Who holds the line
Who are the ones who will die
And feint and sway
As the rook draws in
Who plays with time
And leaps across squares of life
Between glasses and a shot of prose
Who drinks the bitter potion
And plays with the pain of bile
At the break of dawn
Who lives on the roça, *no one knows where*
And why they don't hide
Glimpsing death's pathways
Who bites the rope without breaking it
And warms his hands on the reins of time
Slowly, they come when least expected
Who folds along the diagonal
And moves from black to white
Red mantle, green mount

What spring loses and gains
With cunning yes and force no
Who wakes up to spit at the new day
Who leaps across drawn lines
And rides the saddle of uncertainty
Bewitched herdsman, immune to defeat,
Who quenches the hunger for courage
And spreads a light, constant and wandering
Who guides, guides.

Daniel Brasil

About the Author

Antônio Bispo dos Santos was born in 1959 in the Berlengas River Valley, Piauí. A landworker, he was educated by the knowledge of elders in the Saco Curtume Quilombo in the town of São João do Piauí, and was the first person in his family to learn to read and write. From an early age, he was entrusted with the task of articulating his people's wisdom in writing and mediating their relationship with the State, whose violence includes the delegitimation of oral traditions.

As a community leader, he was active in the State Coordination of Quilombola Communities of Piauí (CECOQ/PI) and in the National Coordination for the Articulation of Black Rural Quilombola Communities (CONAQ). His political work in the movement for land rights was rooted in the worldview of counter-colonial peoples.

Nêgo Bispo, as he was also called, was the author of several articles, poems, and the book *Colonização, Quilombos: modos e significações* (Colonization, Quilombos: Ways and Meanings, UnB/InCTI, 2015). He also coordinated the *Quatro Cantos* (Four Corners) collection (n-1 edições, 2022). His essays "Modos quilombolas" (*Quilombola* Ways, 2016) and "Somos da terra" (We Belong to the Land, 2018) were published in the magazine *PISEAGRAMA*. He delivered lectures, talks, and courses across Brazil. He was a guest professor in the Meeting of Knowledges program at UnB/InCTI and in the Transversal Training in Traditional Knowledge program at the Federal University of Minas Gerais (UFMG).

About the Artist

Santídio Pereira was born in 1996 in the village of Curral Comprido, in the town of Isaías Coelho in the Piauí countryside. He migrated to São Paulo as a child and enrolled in Instituto Acaia, an organization dedicated to children and adolescents living near CEAGESP, the São Paulo wholesale food market, where he began his artistic practice in the Institute's studios.

Woodcut printing is the primary medium of his visual research, through which he has developed the technique of "incision, cutting, and fitting," subverting traditional printmaking's mode of reproduction by using multiple blocks to create a single image. The flora and fauna of the Caatinga biome, and birds in particular, are recurring sources of memory, study, and fictional reinvention in his work. He does research in the Caatinga region of Piauí and has an artist residency project for local residents geared at fostering exchange with visiting artists.